Sophia, God & A Short Tale
About the Antichrist

VLADIMIR SOLOVYOV

SOPHIA, GOD

&

A SHORT TALE ABOUT THE ANTICHRIST

Also Including

At the Dawn of Mist-Shrouded Youth

Translated and Edited
by
BORIS JAKIM

First published in the USA
by Semantron Press
an imprint of Angelico Press 2014
© Boris Jakim 2014

For information, address:
Angelico Press, Ltd.
4709 Briar Knoll Dr. Kettering, OH 45429
www.angelicopress.com

Paperback: 978-1-62138-095-5

Cover image: Diego Velázquez,
St. John on Patmos (detail), 1619–1620

Cover design: Michael Schrauzer

CONTENTS

Editor's Note

THIS VOLUME CONTAINS several late works of Solovyov, representing his final speculations about matters crucial to the final destiny of humanity and the world. As Solovyov's life was coming to an end with the end of the 19th century, his thoughts were directed at three things: the end of the world (the Antichrist), the beauty and wisdom of the world (Sophia), and the nature of God. These works can be said to represent his "last discourse."

The translation of "The Short Tale about the Antichrist" is new and has a new Translator's Introduction. The translations of "At the Dawn of Mist-Shrouded Youth," "Letters to Ekaterina Romanova," "Three Meetings," and "The Concept of God" were published previously, and are given here in slightly revised versions. New Editor's Notes are provided for "Three Meetings" and "The Concept of God," and the earlier Translator's Introduction for "At the Dawn of Mist-Shrouded Youth with Selected Letters to Ekaterina Romanova" has been slightly revised.

All the footnotes in this volume are mine, except where indicated.

BORIS JAKIM

A Short Tale
about the Antichrist

Translator's Foreword

VLADIMIR SOLOVYOV finished the "Short Tale about the Antichrist" just before his death in 1900, and considered it his last testament. It is unlike anything else he wrote, and is the most mystical of his works; the inhabitation of the Antichrist by Satan is one of the most uncanny and unsettling mystical passages in modern literature. This tale is also one of Solovyov's most autobiographical works: many of the Antichrist's attributes—his intellectual genius, his love of humankind, perhaps his pride—are those of Solovyov himself.

The "Short Tale about the Antichrist" appears as the conclusion of a larger work, a series of dialogues entitled *Three Conversations on War, Progress, and the End of Universal History* (1899–1900). The five speakers in these conversations—a General, a Politician, a Prince, a Lady, and Mr. Z.—represent different elements of the Russian intelligentsia, and are chiefly concerned with expounding different views on the struggle against evil and the meaning of history in the light of this struggle. In these conversations Solovyov's view is expressed by Mr. Z. (and by Father Pansophius, the writer of the Antichrist tale, who entrusts Mr. Z. with its manuscript). For Mr. Z., the struggle against evil has a metaphysical meaning and will ultimately be played out on the eschatological plane, as depicted in the Antichrist tale. Much of the Tale is taken from the Book of Revelation, often with exact correspondence of events. The Tale is set in a futuristic 21st century, portrayed as an epoch of technological wonders inconceivable to people of Solovyov's time. In this respect it resembles books like H. G. Wells' *War of the Worlds* and *The Time Machine*, also written at the end of the 19th century.

The Antichrist in Solovyov's tale is kind-hearted and loves humanity. He institutes universal peace and ends hunger. What else do human beings need? Elder John tells him: "we are prepared to receive all good things [from you] if in your generous hand we recognize Christ's holy hand. As for your question, What can I do for you?—here is our direct answer: Confess before us now Jesus Christ, the Son of God, who came in the flesh and rose from the dead, and who will come again. Confess Him, and we will lovingly accept you as the true forerunner of His second and glorious coming." The Antichrist refuses, and all hell breaks out.

A question arises: did Solovyov believe that the events described in the Tale would really occur in some form, if not literally? Or was he trying to find a way to represent some great event that was occurring, or would occur, in the spiritual world that parallels and grounds our earthly world? One way to put it might be that he heard a music coming from the other world and that, practically on his death-bed, he tried to put it into words. Or that he felt the thunder and lightning that were sent from the other world to strike down John and Peter, and heard the tormented underground din coming from the "cupola of souls." The holy geography of Jerusalem and of Palestine was the dwelling place of Solovyov's soul as he was writing the Tale. Andrey Bely's testimony suggests that, very much like John, the author of the Book of the Revelation, Solovyov, at the end, was gazing into the spiritual world and being consumed like a candle by what he saw.[1]

1. The nineteen-year-old Bely was present at a Solovyov family gathering in the spring of 1900 where Solovyov read the "Tale about the Antichrist." This is what Bely saw: "Solovyov was sitting sad and weary, with that imprint of deathly and frightening majesty which rested on him in his last months; it was as if he had seen what no one else had ever seen, and as if he could not find the words to express his knowledge... At the words 'Elder

A Short Tale
about the Antichrist

Pan-Mongolism! Although the word
Is strange, it caresses my hearing
As though it were filled
With premonition of some mighty Divine fate...[2]

A LADY—Where does this epigraph come from?[3]

MR. Z.—I think the author of the tale composed it.

A LADY—Well, read.

MR. Z. (*reads*)—The twentieth century AD was the epoch of the last great wars, internecine conflicts, and revolutions. The remote cause of the greatest of the external wars was the intellectual movement called "pan-Mongolism," which arose in Japan at the end of the nineteenth century. The Japanese, who were adept at imitating and had with amazing rapidity and

---

John rose like a white candle,' he too rose, drawing himself erect in his armchair. Lightning was flashing in the window and Solovyov's face was trembling in a lightning of inspiration" (from the memoir of Solovyov in *Arabeski*, Moscow, 1911).

2. From Solovyov's poem "Pan-Mongolism." This poem alludes to the fear that at the end of the 19th century Russia—because the Russian Orthodox Church had forsaken the law of love—would be destroyed by divine wrath in the form of the "yellow peril."

3. As explained in the Translator's Foreword, "A Short Tale about the Antichrist" is the concluding section of a series of conversations between representative members of the Russian intelligentsia, including "a Lady" and "Mr. Z." The manuscript of the Tale was given to Mr. Z. by a friend of his, the monk Pansophius.

success adopted the material forms of European culture, also assimilated certain European ideas of a lower order. Having learned from newspapers and history textbooks about the existence in the West of pan-Hellenism, pan-Germanism, pan-Slavism, and pan-Islamism, they proclaimed the great idea of pan-Mongolism, i.e., the unification under their leadership of all the nations of Eastern Asia for the purpose of waging a decisive war against the foreigners, i.e., the Europeans. Taking advantage of the fact that at the beginning of the twentieth century Europe was engaged in waging a final decisive war against the Islamic world, the Japanese set out to fulfill their great plan: they occupied Korea and then Peking, where with the aid of the progressive Chinese party they overthrew the old Manchu dynasty and replaced it with a new Japanese dynasty.

The Chinese conservatives soon accepted this state of affairs. They understood that it is better to choose the lesser of two evils, and that, despite everything, the invaders were their brothers. It would have been impossible to preserve the independence of old China as a *state*, and it would inevitably have had to submit either to the Europeans or to the Japanese. It was clear, however, that Japan's dominion, though it abolished the external forms of the Chinese state (forms that had obviously become worthless), did not affect the inner principles of the national life, whereas the hegemony of the European powers, which for political reasons supported the Christian missionaries, threatened the deepest spiritual foundations of China. The former Chinese hatred of the Japanese had developed when neither of them knew the Europeans; but, confronted with the European threat, the hostility of these two kindred nations amounted to an internecine conflict and lost all meaning. The Europeans were *completely* alien, enemies and *nothing else*; and their dominion could not flatter ethnic pride in any way, whereas in Japan's hands the Chinese saw the sweet lure of pan-Mongolism, which in their eyes also justified the sad inevitability of external Europeanization.

"Our dear stubborn brothers, you have to understand," the Japanese insisted, "that we are using the weapons of the western dogs not because we like them, but in order to smash them with those same weapons. If you unite with us and accept our practical guidance, we will soon not only drive the white devils out of our Asia, but we will carry the war into their own countries and establish a true Middle Kingdom over the whole world. You are right in your national pride and in your contempt for the Europeans, but you uselessly nourish these feelings with dreams alone, rather than with rational activity. We are far ahead of you in this activity and must show you the ways leading to our common advantage. You can easily see what you have achieved by a policy of self-reliance and of mistrust of us, your natural friends and protectors: Russia and England, Germany and France, have divided practically all of you among themselves, and all your tiger intentions amount to nothing more than the impotent tip of a snake's tail."

The reasonable Chinese found these arguments justified, and the Japanese dynasty became firmly established. Its first task was, of course, the formation of a powerful army and navy. The greater part of the Japanese military forces were transferred to China, where they served as the basis for an enormous new army. Chinese-speaking Japanese officers proved to be much more competent as instructors than the Europeans they had supplanted, and in the immense populations of China, including Manchuria, Mongolia, and Tibet, there was more than enough suitable military material. The first emperor of the Japanese dynasty conducted a successful test of the weaponry of the revived empire by expelling the French from Tonkin and

Siam, and the English from Burma, and then incorporating all of Indochina into the Middle Empire. His successor—Chinese on his mother's side and thus combining Chinese cunning and adaptability with Japanese energy and ingenuity—mobilized a four-million-man army in Chinese Turkestan; and while Tsun-Li-Yamin was confidentially informing the Russian ambassador that this army was assembled in order to conquer India, the emperor invaded our Central Asia and raised the whole population against us; he then quickly moved across the Urals and inundated with his regiments all of Eastern and Central Russia, while hastily mobilized Russian forces were streaming from Poland and Lithuania, Kiev and Volyn, Petersburg and Finland.

In the absence of a ready war plan, and given the enormous numerical superiority of the enemy, the Russian forces, with all their war-fighting capabilities, could achieve nothing more than death with honor. The rapidity of the invasion did not leave time for the necessary concentration of forces, and the Russian regiments were annihilated one after another in furious and hopeless battles. The victories of the Mongols were not won cheaply, but having gained control of all the Asian railroads, they easily brought in more troops. Meantime, a two-hundred-thousand-man Russian army, which for some time had been assembled at the Manchurian frontier, futilely attempted to invade well-defended China. Having left a portion of his forces in Russia to hinder the formation of a new Russian army as well as to pursue the numerous partisan groups, the emperor crossed the frontiers of Germany with three armies. Germany had had time to prepare, and one of the Mongol armies was destroyed totally. But at this time the party of belated *revanche*[4] gained

---

4. The party of revenge for the humiliating defeat suffered in the Franco-Prussian War.

control of the French government, and a million enemy bayo-
nets soon appeared at the rear of the Germans. Caught between
a hammer and an anvil, the German army was forced to accept
the honorable conditions of disarmament offered by the
emperor. The jubilant French, fraternizing with the yellow-
faced invaders, scattered over Germany and soon lost all conception of military discipline. The emperor ordered his armies
to slaughter the no-longer-needed allies, which they did with
the usual Chinese precision. Meanwhile, in Paris, workers *sans
patrie* staged a revolt, and the capital of western culture joyfully
opened its gates to the ruler of the East. Having satisfied his
curiosity, the emperor traveled to Boulogne-sur-Mer, where,
protected by a fleet that had come from the Pacific, transport
ships were being prepared to take his armies to Great Britain.
But he needed money, and the English bought him off with a
billion pounds. After a year, all the European states acknowledged themselves to be vassals of the emperor, who, having left
a sufficient occupying army in Europe, returned to the East and
organized naval expeditions to America and Australia.[5]

The new Mongol yoke over Europe lasted for half a century. The inner life of this epoch was marked by a ubiquitous
mixing and profound interpenetration of European and Eastern
ideas, by the repetition *en grand* of the ancient Alexandrian syn-
cretism. The practical realms of life were primarily characterized by three phenomena: the large-scale migration into Europe
of Chinese and Japanese laborers and the consequent intensifi-
cation of the socio-economic question; the continuing palliative
attempts on the part of the ruling classes to resolve this question; and the increased international activity of secret societies

---

5. An interesting prefiguration of Pearl Harbor and of the war in the
Pacific.

organizing a vast all-European conspiracy for the purpose of expelling the Mongols and reestablishing European independence.

This colossal conspiracy, in which the local national governments also participated to the extent they could evade the control of the emperor's deputies, was organized masterfully and succeeded brilliantly. At the appointed hour the massacre of the Mongol soldiers began, along with the slaughter and expulsion of the Asian laborers. Secret armies emerged all over Europe, and a universal mobilization took place in accordance with a detailed plan prepared long in advance. The new emperor, a grandson of the great conqueror, hastened from China to Russia, but his countless regiments were smashed by the all-European army. Their scattered remnants returned into the depths of Asia, and Europe became free.

If the half-century subjugation by the Asian barbarians took place because of the disunification of states that thought only of their individual national interests, the great and glorious liberation was achieved by the international organization of the unified forces of the entire European population. As a natural consequence of this obvious fact, the old, traditional order of individual nations lost its validity, and the last remnants of the old monarchic institutions disappeared almost everywhere. In the twenty-first century, Europe constituted a union of more or less democratic states—a European united states. The successes of external culture, somewhat delayed by the Mongol invasion and the struggle for liberation, resumed their accelerated pace. However, matters of inner consciousness—questions of life and death, of the final destiny of the world and man, complicated and tangled by a multitude of new physiological and psychological investigations and discoveries—remained, as before, unresolved. Only one important negative result was clear: theoretical materialism was bankrupt. The idea that the universe was a system of dancing atoms and that life was the result of a mechanical accumulation of infinitesimal changes of matter—this idea could no longer satisfy any thinking mind. Humankind had outgrown forever this stage of philosophical infancy. But it was clear, on the other hand, that it had also outgrown the infantile capacity for naïve, unquestioning faith. Such concepts as a God who had created the world out of nothing and so on, were no longer taught even in the elementary schools. A certain general high level of ideas about such objects had been worked out, below which no dogmatism could sink. And if the overwhelming majority of thinking people were no longer believers, the few remaining believers all necessarily became *thinking* people, fulfilling the apostle's commandment: be children at heart, but not in mind.

Among the few believer-spiritualists there lived at this time a remarkable man—many called him a superman—who was far from being a child, either in mind or in heart. He was still young, but thanks to his extraordinary genius he had by age thirty-three gained wide fame as a great thinker, writer, and public figure. Conscious of the great power of spirit in himself, he was always a confirmed spiritualist, and his clear mind always showed him the truth of what one should believe in: the Good, God, the Messiah. That is what he *believed* in, but he *loved only himself.* He believed in God, but in the depths of his soul he involuntarily and unconsciously preferred himself to God. He believed in the Good, but Eternity's all-seeing eye knew that this man would worship the power of evil if it ever undertook to buy him—not by the snare of the senses and base passions, and not even with the allurement of power, but through unbounded pride alone. However, this pride was neither an unconscious instinct nor an insane pretension. Even apart from his exceptional genius, beauty, and nobility of character, it seemed that the abstinence, unselfishness, and active charity that he manifested to the highest degree were sufficient to justify the enormous pride of this great spiritualist, ascetic, and philanthropist. And can one blame him, upon whom God's gifts were so abundantly bestowed, that he should see in them special signs of being exceptionally favored from above and consider himself second after God, a son of God unique of his kind? In short, he considered himself to be what Christ really was. But this consciousness of his high worth was manifested in him not as moral duty toward God and the world, but as a sense that he was privileged with greater rights than other men and that he was even superior to Christ. At first he did not have any enmity toward Jesus. He acknowledged His messianic significance and dignity, but honestly saw in Him only his own greatest precursor; Christ's moral feat and His absolute uniqueness were incomprehensible for this pride-darkened mind.

"Christ came before me," he reasoned. "I come second, but that which comes later in the order of time is, in essence, more primary. I come last, at the end of history, precisely because I am the perfect and definitive savior. That Christ was my forerunner. His mission was to prepare the way for my coming." Reasoning thus, the great man of the twenty-first century will apply to himself everything the Gospel says about the second coming, explaining this coming not as the return of that same Christ, but as the replacement of the preliminary Christ by the definitive one, that is, by the great man himself.

At this stage, the man who has come is not yet unique or original. For example, Mohammed viewed his relation to Christ in the same way, but Mohammed was a righteous man who could not be accused of any evil intentions.

This man will also use another argument to justify his prideful preference of himself to Christ: "Preaching the moral good and manifesting it in his life, Christ was a *reformer* of humankind, whereas I am called to be the *benefactor* of this partly reformed and partly unreformable humankind. To all people I will give all that is necessary. Christ, as a moralist, divided people according to good and evil, whereas I will unite them by benefits that are needed by the good and the evil alike. I will be the true representative of that God whose sun shines on the good and the evil alike, whose rain falls equally on the just and on the unjust. Christ brought a sword; I will bring peace. He threatened the earth with a terrible last judgment. But I will be the last judge, and my judgment will be not only a judgment of justice but also a judgment of mercy. There will be justice in my judgment, but it will be a distributive justice, not a punitive one. I will differentiate among all persons and give to each what he needs."

And in this exalted frame of mind he awaits some clear summons from God to begin his work of the new salvation of humankind; he awaits some obvious and astonishing sign that he is God's eldest son, the beloved first-born. He waits and nourishes his selfhood with the consciousness of his superhuman virtues and gifts, for, as has been said, he is a man of irreproachable morality and extraordinary genius.

This proud, righteous man awaits higher sanction that will permit him to begin his salvation of humankind—but it does not come. He is already thirty years old, and then three more years pass. Suddenly the thought dawns in his mind and pierces the marrow of his bones like a hot spasm: "What if? What if I am not the one, but he, the Galilean, was the one? What if he is not my forerunner, but the true one, first and last? But then he must be *alive*... Where is he? What if he comes to me, here and now? What will I say to him? Would I have to bow down to the ground before him like the most abject and stupid of Christians, like some Russian peasant, and mutter meaninglessly: 'Lord Jesus Christ, have mercy upon me, a sinner'? Or, like a Polish peasant woman, would I have to flatten myself before him like a pancake? No, never! I am a luminous genius, a superman."

And here, in place of the former cold rational respect for God and Christ, there were born and grew in his heart first a kind of horror, then a burning envy consuming his entire being, and finally a vehement, venomous hatred. "I am the one, I; not he! He is not alive, and never will be. He did not rise from the dead, did not rise, did not rise! He is rotting, rotting in his tomb, rotting like the last..."

His mouth foaming, he rushed out of his house hopping convulsively and ran out of his garden into the pitch-black night on a path over cliffs... His fury subsided and was replaced by an arid, heavy despair as forbidding as those cliffs and as somber as that night. He stopped before a sheer precipice and heard the muffled sound of a stream flowing over rocks far below. An unbearable anguish ate at his heart. Suddenly something stirred within him.

"Should I call him and ask him what I should do?" And in the midst of the darkness he seemed to see a meek and sorrowful figure. "He pities me... No, never! He did not rise, did not rise!" And he threw himself off the precipice. But something buoyant, like a water spout, held him up in the air; he felt a convulsion like that from an electric shock, and some force threw him back onto the cliff. He lost consciousness for an instant; when he revived, he found himself kneeling a few paces from the precipice. Before him he saw a figure shining with a misty phosphorescent glow, and its two eyes pierced his soul with an unbearably sharp light... He saw those two piercing eyes and heard—whether inside himself or outside, he did not know—a strange voice, hollow and muffled, yet also distinct, metallic, and completely soulless, as if coming from a phonograph.

And this voice said to him: "My beloved son, in you I am well pleased. Why did you not seek me? Why did you worship the other one, the bad one, and his father? I am your god and father. The other one, the crucified beggar, is alien to me and to you. I have no son except you. You are my only begotten son, equal to me. I love you and do not ask anything of you. Even without that, you are beautiful, great, and powerful. Do your work in *your own* name, not mine. I have no envy toward you. I love you. I do not need anything from you. The one you regarded as god, he demanded obedience from his son, absolute obedience, unto the death on the cross; and he did not help him on the cross. I do not demand anything from you, and I will help you. For the sake of you yourself, for the sake of your personal dignity and superiority, and for the sake of my pure, selfless love for you—I will help you. Receive my spirit. Even as before my spirit begot you in *beauty*, so now it begets you in *power*."

With these words of the unknown one, the superman's lips opened involuntarily, the two piercing eyes came very close to his face, and he felt a sharp icy breath enter him and fill his entire being. At the same time he felt an unprecedented power, boldness, lightness, and ecstasy. At that instant the glowing figure and the two eyes suddenly disappeared, and something lifted the superman above the ground and immediately brought him down in his garden, by the doors of his house.

The next day visitors of the great man, and even his servants, were startled by his unusual, inspired look. But they would have been even more astonished if they could have seen with what supernatural rapidity and ease he wrote, after locking himself in his study, his famous work, *The Open Path to Universal Peace and Prosperity*.

The superman's previous books and public activity had always encountered severe critics, although for the most part these critics were deeply religious men who thus lacked all authority (this was the time of the coming of the Antichrist, after all), and therefore few people listened to them when they pointed out that everything the "man who has come" wrote and said was marked by an intense and exceptional pride and conceit, and by the absence of true simplicity, sincerity, and feeling.

But with this new work he will convince even some of his previous critics and opponents. This book, written after the adventure on the cliff, will display in him a unprecedented power of genius. It will embrace and reconcile all contradictions. It will unite a noble veneration of ancient traditions and symbols with a broad and bold radicalism of socio-political demands and guidance; an unlimited freedom of thought with the profoundest understanding of all that is mystical; unconditional individualism with fervent devotion to the common good; and the sublimest idealism of guiding principles with the complete concreteness and vitality of practical solutions. All this will be unified by such brilliant art that every one-sided thinker or political activist will easily see and accept in it the whole from his own particular point of view, without making any sacrifices for the *truth itself*, without truly transcending for it his *own I*, without *really* renouncing his own one-sidedness, without correcting the error of his own opinions and aspirations, without in any way remedying their deficiencies.

This astonishing book will immediately be translated into the languages of all the educated nations, and some of the uneducated ones. For a whole year, thousands of newspapers all over the globe will be filled with the publisher's advertisements for this book and ecstatic reviews. Millions of copies of cheap editions with a portrait of the author will be sold, and the whole cultural world (and at that time this will encompass the whole globe) will be filled with the praises of this great, incomparable, unique man! No one will criticize this book; everyone will see in it the revelation of universal and total truth. It will cover the past with such justice, it will evaluate the present so dispassionately and comprehensively, it will portray a better future so clearly and palpably, that everyone will say: "Here is the very thing that we need; here is an ideal that is not utopian; here is a plan that is not chimerical." This wondrous writer will not only captivate everyone, but he will also give pleasure to everyone who receives him, so that Christ's words will be fulfilled:

"I am come in my Father's name, and ye receive me not: if another shall come in his own name, him ye will receive."[6] For in order to be received, one must give pleasure.[7]

True, a few pious people, while enthusiastically praising the book, will ask why Christ is never mentioned, but other Christians will answer: "Thank God, He's not! In past ages, all sorts of zealots had sufficiently manhandled what is holy; at the present time, a profoundly religious writer must be very careful. The book is permeated with a truly Christian spirit of active love and all-embracing goodwill; what more do you need?" And everyone will agree.

Soon after the publication of *The Open Path*, which made its author the most popular man ever to have appeared on earth, an international constituent assembly of the union of European states was to take place in Berlin. This union, established after a series of external and internal wars which had been connected with emancipation from the Mongol yoke and had significantly

6. John 5:43.
7. Play on words in Russian involving byt' priniatym (to be received) and byt' priatnym (to give pleasure, or to be pleasant or agreeable).

changed the map of Europe, was imperiled by new conflicts—now not between nations, but between political and social parties. The powerful brotherhood of Freemasons, who were the force behind the policy of European union, realized that a common executive power was lacking. The European unity, achieved with such difficulty, could at any moment fall apart. The union council, or "universal committee" (*Comité permanent universel*), lacked unanimity, since authentic Masons, who were initiated in the true nature of the matter, had not succeeded in occupying all the seats. Independent members of the council entered into separate agreements with one another, and this augured the threat of a new war. At that point the "initiated" members decided to institute a single executive authority wielding sufficient power.

The main candidate was a secret member of the order—"the man who has come." He was the only man who possessed great universal fame. Having been trained as an artillery officer, and possessing a large fortune from capitalist ventures, he had friends everywhere in financial and military circles. In a less enlightened time his candidacy would have been hampered by the fact that his origins were shrouded in obscurity. His mother, a lady of rather doubtful reputation, was very well known in both of the earth's hemispheres, while a great many men had reason to think they were his father. Of course, these facts could not have any significance for an age so progressive that it was destined to be the last one.

"The man who has come" was elected almost unanimously as president for life of the European United States; and when he appeared on the platform in the full glory of his youthful, superhuman beauty and power, and expounded his universal program with inspired eloquence, in an explosion of enthusiasm the captivated and charmed assembly resolved without voting to bestow upon him the supreme title of Roman emperor. The congress closed with universal rejoicing, and the great chosen one issued a manifesto that began with the words "Nations of the Earth! I give you my peace!" and ended with the words "Nations of the Earth! The promises are fulfilled! Everlasting universal peace is assured. Any attempt to disrupt it will immediately be put down with overwhelming force. From this moment there is on earth a mediating power that is stronger than all other powers, whether taken separately or together. This overwhelming, all-conquering power belongs to me, the fully empowered chosen one of Europe, the emperor of all her forces. International law has finally acquired the sanction it had hitherto lacked. Henceforth no nation will dare to say 'War' when I say 'Peace.' Nations of the Earth, peace to you!"

This manifesto had the desired effect. Everywhere outside of Europe, especially in America, powerful imperialist parties were formed which forced their nations to join the European United States under the supreme authority of the Roman emperor. Here and there, a number of independent tribes and nations still remained in Asia and Africa. With a small but elite army consisting of Russian, German, Polish, Hungarian, and Turkish regiments, the emperor paraded from Eastern Asia to Morocco, and with hardly any bloodshed he subjugated all those who had been recalcitrant. In all the lands of the two halves of the world he installed as his representatives European-educated local leaders who were devoted to him. In all the pagan lands the defeated and enchanted populations proclaimed him as their supreme god. In a single year a universal monarchy in the literal sense had been established. The sprouts of war were eradicated. The Universal League for Peace convened for the last time and, after pronouncing an ecstatic panegyric to the great peacemaker, it abolished itself because it was no longer necessary.

In the new year of his reign the Roman and universal emperor issued a new manifesto: "Nations of the Earth! I promised you peace and I gave it to you. But peace is sweet only if it is combined with prosperity. Peace does not delight those who are threatened with the woes of poverty. Come unto me now all who hunger and are cold, so that I may feed you and give you warmth." He then announced a simple and all-encompassing social reform, which he had already sketched out in his book and which had already captivated all serious and generous minds. Thanks to the fact that he had concentrated in his hands all of the world's finances and all of its wealth and resources, he could now implement a reform that would benefit the poor without appreciably harming the rich. Everyone would receive according to his abilities, and every ability would receive according to its toil and merits.

The new ruler of the earth was above all a kind-hearted philanthropist—and not just a philanthropist but even a "philozoist."[8] He was a vegetarian, prohibited vivisection, and implemented strict supervision over slaughterhouses; he strongly supported all societies for the protection of animals. More important than these details was the fact that he had firmly instituted among all of humankind the most fundamental equality: the *equality of freedom from hunger.* This took place in the second year of his reign. The socio-economic problem was solved conclusively. But if to be fed is the most important thing for hungry people, then people who have been fed want something else as well.

Even animals, after eating, usually want not only to sleep but also to play. Even more so is this true for humankind, which *post panem* always demanded *circenses.*[9]

8. A lover of all forms of life, especially animals.
9. "Which after bread always demanded circuses."

The superman-emperor will understand what his crowd needs. At this time a great magician, shrouded in a thick cloud of strange legends and wild fables, will come to him in Rome from the Far East. According to rumors circulating among the neo-Buddhists,[10] he will be of divine birth—the child of the sun god Surya and some river nymph.

This magician, Apollonius by name, semi-Asiatic and semi-European, a Catholic bishop *in partibus infidelium*, is undoubtedly a man of genius. In an amazing fashion he will combine mastery of the latest achievements and technological applications of western science with knowledge and mastery of what was authentically solid and significant in the traditional mysticism of the East. The results of this combination will be astonishing. Among other things, Apollonius will master the semi-scientific, semi-magical art of employing will power to attract and direct atmospheric electricity, and among the common people it will be said that he "brings fire down from heaven." However, while startling the crowd's imagination with various unheard-of wonders, for a time he will not abuse his power for any particular purpose. So, this man will come to the great emperor, bow down to him as the true son of God, and proclaim that in secret books of the East he has found direct prophecies that he, the emperor, will be the last savior and judge of the world, and he will offer himself and his art at the emperor's service.

Enchanted, the emperor will receive him as a gift from above, and, decorating him with all manner of fancy titles, will from this moment always have him by his side. And now the nations of the Earth, blessed by their lord with all manner of benefits, will receive—in addition to universal peace and universal freedom from hunger—the possibility of never-ending enjoy-

10. Allusion to the Theosophical movement.

ment of the most diverse and unexpected miracles and signs. The third year of the superman's reign was coming to an end.

After the successful resolution of the socio-political problem, the next problem to come to the fore was the religious one. It was raised by the emperor himself, primarily in relation to Christianity. At this time the situation of Christianity was as follows. Its numbers had been reduced very substantially (in the whole world there remained not more than forty-five million Christians), but this allowed it to become morally tighter and more disciplined: it had gained in quality what it had lost in quantity. People who were not connected with Christianity by any spiritual interest were no longer counted as Christians. The various confessions had been reduced fairly proportionately in their numbers, so that more or less the same numerical ratios were maintained between them. As for their feelings toward one another, though the former mutual enmity had not been replaced by total reconciliation, it had grown much more moderate, and the oppositions had lost their former acuteness.

The papacy had long before been expelled from Rome, and after much wandering it was given refuge in Petersburg under the condition that it abstain from propaganda there and elsewhere in the country. In Russia the papacy became greatly simplified: without substantially changing the necessary make-up of its colleges and offices, it had to spiritualize the character of their activity and to reduce to a minimum its sumptuous rituals and ceremonies. Though never formally revoked, many of the papacy's strange and seductive customs were simply dropped. In all other countries, especially in North America, the Catholic hierarchy still had many representatives; with their strength of will, tireless energy, and independence in the community, they were able to achieve a greater unity of the Catholic Church than it had enjoyed in the past and to preserve its international,

cosmopolitan significance. Protestantism, whose leader continued to be Germany, especially after a significant part of the
Anglican Church had united with the Catholic Church, was
cleansed of its extreme negative tendencies, whose adherents
openly adopted religious indifferentism and atheism. In the
Evangelical Church there remained only true believers, whose
leaders combined vast learning with deep religiosity as well as
with an ever-increasing tendency to revive in themselves the
living image of authentic ancient Christianity.

Russian Orthodoxy, though it lost many millions of its
nominal members after political events had changed the official
position of the Church, experienced the joy of union with the
better Old Believers and even with many sectarians of a positive
religious orientation.[11] This renewed Church, though not
growing in numbers, began to grow in strength of spirit, which
it notably showed in its internal struggle against extreme sects
marked by demonic and satanic elements, sects that were rap-
idly spreading among the people and in society.

In the first two years of the new reign, Christians, frightened and wearied by the series of preceding revolutions and
wars, looked upon the new ruler and his peace reforms with a
favorable wait-and-see attitude, or even with unreserved sympathy and fervent enthusiasm. But in the third year, with the
appearance of the great magician, many of the Orthodox, Catholics, and Evangelicals became seriously apprehensive and anti-
pathetic. The Gospel and Apostolic texts that spoke of the
prince of this world and of the Antichrist were read more atten-
tively and explicated more excitedly. The emperor got wind of

11. The "better" Old Believers were those less un-Orthodox in their
doctrines. The Russian sects with a "positive orientation" were those not
characterized by weird erotic and ascetic practices.

the gathering storm and resolved to clarify the matter as soon as possible. At the beginning of the fourth year of his reign he issued a manifesto to all his faithful Christians without distinction as to denomination, inviting them to elect or appoint fully empowered representatives to an ecumenical council under his chairmanship. At that time his residence was moved from Rome to Jerusalem. Palestine was then an autonomous region, populated and governed primarily by Jews. Jerusalem had been free, but now it became an imperial city. The Christian shrines remained untouched, but on the whole wide platform of Haram esh-Sharif—from Birket Israin and the present barracks on one side and up to the Al-Aqsa Mosque and "Solomon's stables" on the other—a huge building was erected, containing, in addition to two small old mosques, a large "imperial" temple for the unification of all cults and two opulent imperial palaces with libraries, museums, and special rooms for magical experiments and exercises.

The ecumenical council was to open in this semi-temple, semi-palace on September 14. Since the Evangelical confession does not have a priesthood in the strict sense, the Catholic and Orthodox hierarchs, in compliance with the emperor's wish to impart a character of uniformity to the representation of all the parts of Christianity, allowed the participation in the council of a certain number of lay persons known for their piety and devotion to church interests; but once lay persons were allowed, it was impossible to exclude the lower clergy, both black and white.[12] Thus, the total number of participants at the council exceeded three thousand, while about half a million Christian pilgrims inundated Jerusalem and all of Palestine.

12. The black are the monastics; the white are the priests who are allowed to marry.

Among the participants at the council, three stood out in particular. First, there was Pope Peter II, who headed the Catholic contingent of the council. His predecessor had died on the way to the council, and in Damascus a conclave was convened that unanimously elected Cardinal Simone Barionini, who took the name Peter. He was of peasant stock, from the Neapolitan region; he had become known as a preacher of the Carmelite order and had been prominent in the struggle against a satanic sect that was flourishing in Petersburg and its environs and seducing not only Orthodox but also Catholics. Having been consecrated first as Archbishop of Mogilev and then as Cardinal, he had early been destined for the tiara. He was about fifty years old, strongly built and of medium height, with a red face, hooked nose, and thick eyebrows. He was excitable and impetuous, spoke with fervor and with sweeping gestures, and tended to captivate rather than convince his listeners. The new pope mistrusted and was ill-disposed toward the universal leader, especially after the late pope, on the way to the council, had yielded to the emperor's insistence and made a cardinal of the imperial chancellor and great universal magician, the exotic bishop Apollonius, whom Peter considered a dubious Catholic and an indubitable deceiver.

The effective, though unofficial, leader of the Orthodox was Elder John, who was very well known among the Russian people. Though he was officially listed as a "retired" bishop, he did not reside in any monastery, but instead constantly wandered in all directions. Various legends circulated about him. Some asserted that he was the reincarnation of Fyodor Kuzmich, i.e., Tsar Alexander I,[13] who was born about three

13. Rumors circulated that Tsar Alexander I did not die in 1825 but became a religious wanderer called Fyodor Kuzmich.

centuries before this. Others went further and asserted that he was the real Elder John, i.e., the apostle John the Divine, who had never died and now openly appeared in the last times. He himself never spoke of his origins or of his youth. He was now a very ancient but vigorous old man with yellowish and even greenish white hair and beard; he was tall and thin but with full and slightly rosy cheeks and lively gleaming eyes; there was extreme kindness in the expression of his face and in the words he spoke; he always wore a white vestment and cloak.

The Evangelical participants were headed by Professor Ernst Pauli, a German theologian of immense learning. He was a short, wizened old man with an enormous forehead, sharp nose, and well-shaven chin. His eyes were marked by a furiously kind gaze. He was constantly rubbing his hands together, shaking his head, twitching his eyebrows, and violently opening and closing his mouth; as he did this, his eyes would gleam and he would abruptly and gloomily emit the words: "So! nun! ja! so also!" He was dressed with formal solemnity—in white tie and a long pastoral dress-coat with certain honorary insignias.

The opening of the council was impressive. Two thirds of the enormous temple devoted to the "unity of all cults" was filled with benches and other kinds of seats for the council participants, while one third was taken up by a high stage where, in addition to the emperor's throne and another throne, on a lower elevation, for the great magician who was also a cardinal and imperial chancellor—in addition to this there were rows of armchairs in the back for ministers, courtiers, and secretaries, while along the side there were longer rows of armchairs whose purpose was unknown. The galleries were occupied by orchestras, while in the adjoining square two Guards regiments were assembled and cannons set up for celebratory salvos. The council participants had already celebrated their services in their various churches, and the opening of the council was to be completely secular in character.

When the emperor entered accompanied by his retinue and by the great magician, the orchestra started playing the "March of One Humankind," the imperial international hymn; at that point all council participants rose to their feet and, waving their hats, shouted thrice: "Vivat! Ura! Hoch!" Standing next to his throne and stretching forward his hand with majestic benevolence, the emperor proclaimed in a sonorous and pleasing voice: "Christians of all confessions! My beloved subjects and brothers! From the beginning of my reign, which the Supreme Being has blessed with such wondrous and glorious works, I have never had occasion to be dissatisfied with you. You have always fulfilled your duty faithfully and conscientiously. But that is not enough for me. My sincere love for you, beloved brothers, thirsts for reciprocity. My desire is that you will be compelled not by a sense of duty but by a sense of heartfelt love to recognize me as your true leader in all works undertaken for the good of humankind. And so, besides the things I do for all people, I desire to grant you special favors. Christians, how can I make you happy? What can I give you, not as my subjects, but as my co-believers and brothers? Christians! Tell me what you find most precious in Christianity so that I could direct all my efforts to that end."

He stopped and waited. A muffled hubbub passed through the temple. The council participants were whispering among themselves. Pope Peter, gesticulating excitedly, was telling his companions something. Professor Pauli was shaking his head and furiously smacking his lips. Elder John, bent over an eastern bishop and a capuchin, was quietly lecturing them. After waiting for a few minutes, the emperor addressed the council again with the same caressing tone, but now there was a barely perceptible

note of irony in it: "Dear Christians," he said. "I know how difficult it is for you to give me a single direct answer. I want to help
you with that too. Unfortunately, since ancient times you have
been divided into so many different denominations and parties
that you perhaps lack a single common center of gravity. But
even if you cannot agree among yourselves, I hope to bring all
your parties into agreement by bestowing upon them an equal
love and an equal readiness to fulfill the *true* aspiration of each.
Dear Christians! I know that for many of you, and not the least
among you, the most precious thing in Christianity is the *spiritual authority* it gives to its lawful representatives—not for their
personal benefit, of course, but for the common good, since this
authority is the basis of the correct spiritual order and moral discipline that is necessary for all. Dear Catholic brothers! Oh, how
I understand your view, and how I would like to base my rule on
the authority of your spiritual head! Lest you think this mere
flattery and empty words, we proclaim solemnly: in accordance
with our sovereign will, the supreme bishop of all Catholics, the
pope of Rome, is henceforth restored to his throne in Rome with
all the former rights and privileges appertaining to this title and
office that had ever been bestowed by our predecessors, beginning with Emperor Constantine the Great. From you, my Catholic brothers, the only thing I desire in return is that you
acknowledge me in your hearts as your sole patron and protec-
tor. Those who acknowledge me as such in conscience and feeling, let them come here to me."

He pointed to the empty seats on the stage. Exclaiming joyfully "Gratias agimus! Domine! Salvum fac magnum impera-
torum,"[14] almost all the princes of the Catholic Church, the

14. "We give thanks! Lord! Long live the great emperor!" (The beginning is adapted from the *Gloria* of the Catholic mass.)

cardinals and bishops, as well as the majority of the lay Catholics present, and more than half of the monks, climbed up on the stage and, after bowing low to the emperor, sat down in their armchairs. But down below, in the middle of the council, Pope Peter II sat erect and motionless, like a marble statue. All who had been sitting around him were now on the stage. But a sparse crowd of monks and lay persons who had remained below moved close to him, forming a tight circle around him; and from there one heard the low whisper: "Non praevalebunt, non praevalebunt portae inferni."[15]

Looking with astonishment at the motionless pope, the emperor addressed the assembly in a loud voice: "Dear brothers! I know that among you there are also those for whom the most precious thing in Christianity is its *sacred tradition*, the old symbols, the old hymns and prayers, the icons and liturgical rites. And, truly, what can be more precious than this for a religious soul? Know, then, my beloved ones, that today I signed the charter and allocated ample resources for establishment of a Universal Museum of Christian Archeology in our glorious imperial city of Constantinople with the aim of collecting, studying, and preserving diverse monuments of Christian antiquity, especially from the Eastern churches. I request that tomorrow you elect from your members a commission to discuss with me the measures that should be taken in order to bring our contemporary way of life, mores, and customs closer to the traditions and institutions of the Holy Orthodox Church! My Orthodox brothers! Those who are gladdened by this desire of

---

15. From Matthew 16:18: *Tu es Petrus, et super hanc petram aedificabo Ecclesiam meam, et portae inferi non praevalebunt adversus eam.* ("Thou art Peter, and upon this rock I will build my church; and the gates of hell shall not prevail against it.")

mine and who in their hearts can call me their true leader and lord, let them come up here to me."

The majority of the hierarchs of the East and North, half of the Old Believers, and more than half of the Orthodox priests, monks, and laity climbed up on the stage with joyful shouts, throwing sidelong glances at the Catholics proudly sitting there already. But Elder John did not move, and was sighing loudly. And when the crowd around him grew very sparse, he left his bench and sat closer to Pope Peter and his circle. He was followed by other Orthodox who had not climbed up onto the stage.

The emperor spoke again: "I know, my dear Christians, that there are also those among you for whom the most precious thing in Christianity is personal assurance in the truth, and the free investigation, of Scripture. There is no need for me to elaborate my own view of this. You perhaps know that in my youth I wrote a large book on Biblical criticism that was a bit of a sensation and marked the beginning of my fame. And just a few days ago, probably as a remembrance of this work, the University of Tübingen sent me a request to accept from it an honorary doctorate of theology. I answered that I would accept it with pleasure and gratitude. Meanwhile, today, in addition to the Museum of Christian Archeology, I signed the charter for a universal institute for the free investigation of Holy Scripture in all its possible aspects and orientations, and for the study of all related sciences, with an annual budget of one and a half million marks. Those whose souls are gladdened by this heartfelt initiative of mine and who can with genuine feeling acknowledge me as their lord and ruler, let them come up here to the new doctor of theology."

The great man's golden mouth was slightly distorted by a strange smile. More than half of the learned theologians moved toward the stage, although they did not hurry and were clearly wavering. They were all looking back at Professor Pauli, who sat as if rooted to his seat. His head was lowered, his body bent and twisted. The theologians who had climbed up onto the stage were confused, and suddenly one of them shook his head, jumped off the stage and, limping, ran back to Professor Pauli and the remnant that stayed with him. Professor Pauli raised his head, rose in a somewhat contorted way, walked past the empty benches, accompanied by his co-believers who stayed with him, and sat down closer to Elder John and Pope Peter with their circles.

A large majority of the council, including almost the entire hierarchy of the East and West, was now sitting on the stage. Only three groups remained below: they had formed tight circles around Elder John, Pope Peter, and Professor Pauli, and sat close to one another.

The emperor addressed them in melancholy tones: "What more can I do for you? Strange people! What do you want from me? I do not know. Tell me yourselves, you Christians who have been deserted by the majority of your brothers and leaders and condemned by popular sentiment: what is the most precious thing for you in Christianity?" Here, Elder John rose like a white candle and answered meekly: "Great emperor! The most precious thing for us in Christianity is Christ himself—he himself, and from him comes everything, for we know that 'in him dwelleth all the fullness of the Godhead bodily.'[16] But from you too, emperor, we are prepared to receive all good things, if in your generous hand we recognize Christ's holy hand. As for your question, What can I do for you?—here is our direct answer: Confess before us now Jesus Christ, the Son of God, who came in the flesh and rose from the dead, and who will

16. Colossians 2:9.

come again. Confess him, and we will lovingly accept you as the true forerunner of his second and glorious coming."

He stopped speaking and stared at the emperor's face. Something evil was happening to the emperor. Inside him a storm out of hell was raging, very much like the one he had experienced on that fatal night at the precipice. He had completely lost his internal equilibrium, and he concentrated all his thoughts on maintaining his external composure so as not to give himself away before it was time. He was making a superhuman effort to refrain from throwing himself with a savage cry on the speaker and ripping him apart with his teeth. Suddenly he heard a familiar, unearthly voice: "Be silent and fear nothing." He was silent. But his deathly, darkened face was completely contorted and light was flashing from his eyes.

Meantime, while Elder John was speaking, the great magician, who was sitting wrapped in his enormous tricolored cloak, which covered his cardinal's purple, seemed to be conducting some sort of manipulations beneath it, his eyes flashing intensely and his lips moving. One could see through the open windows of the temple that an enormous black cloud had gathered, and soon everything grew dark. Elder John kept staring with amazed and frightened eyes at the face of the silent emperor, and suddenly he recoiled in horror and, turning around, shouted in a voice stifled with torment: "My children, this is the Antichrist!" At this time, following a deafening thunderclap, an enormous bolt of circular lightning exploded in the temple, enveloping the Elder. Everything was still for a moment, and by the time the thunderstruck Christians had regained their senses, Elder John lay dead.

The emperor, pale but calm, addressed the assembly: "You have witnessed God's judgment. I did not desire anyone's death, but my Father in heaven wreaks vengeance for his beloved son.

The matter is decided. Who will argue with the Most High? Secretaries! Write this down: 'The ecumenical council of all Christians, after the fire from heaven had slain the mad opponent of the divine majesty, unanimously recognized as its supreme leader and lord the sovereign emperor of Rome and of the whole world.'"

Suddenly a single loud and distinct word roared through the temple: "Contradicitur." Pope Peter II rose, and with crimson face and shaking with wrath he raised his staff toward the emperor: "Our only Lord is Jesus Christ, the Son of the living God. As for who you are—you have heard. Get thee hence, Cain, brother-murderer! Get thee hence, devil's vessel! By the power of Christ, I, servant of the servants of God, expel you, filthy dog, forever from God's home and proffer you to your father, Satan! Anathema, anathema, anathema!"

While Pope Peter spoke, the great magician was agitatedly performing his manipulations beneath his cloak; and louder than the last anathema was the thunder, and the last pope fell dead. "That is how all my foes will perish at my father's hand," cried the emperor. "Pereant, pereant,"[17] shouted the trembling princes of the church. He turned and, leaning on the great magician's shoulder and accompanied by his whole crowd, exited slowly at the back of the stage. In the temple remained only the two corpses and a tight circle of Christians half-dead from fear. Professor Pauli was the only one who kept his head. The common horror seemed to awaken in him all the powers of his spirit. He was changed outwardly too: his appearance became majestic and inspired. With decisive strides he ascended the stage, sat down in one the seats previously occupied by a secretary, took a sheet of paper, and began to write something on it.

17. "Let them perish, let them perish."

After finishing, he rose and read in a thunderous voice: "The ecumenical council of God's churches gathered in Jerusalem to the glory of our one Savior, Jesus Christ, this council—after our most blessed brother John, the leader of eastern Christianity, exposed the great deceiver and foe of God as being the true Antichrist foretold by the Word of God, and after our most blessed father Peter, the leader of western Christianity, lawfully and justly proferred him to endless separation from God's church—this council now decrees—before the bodies of these two martyrs of Christ murdered for the truth—the following: to cease all relations with the outcast and his foul minions, and to withdraw into the wilderness to await there the imminent coming of our true Lord, Jesus Christ." Great excitement possessed the crowd, which shouted loudly: "Adveniat! Adveniat cito! Komm Herr Jesu, komm! Come, Lord Jesus!"

Professor Pauli wrote the following at the end of the decree and read it: "Having accepted unanimously this first and last act of the last ecumenical council, we sign our names." And he invited those present to sign. They all hurriedly ascended the stage and signed. At the end he signed in large Gothic script: "Duorum defunctorum testium locum tenes Ernst Pauli."[18] "Let us now go with our ark of the last covenant!" he said, pointing to the two dead martyrs. The bodies were lifted onto stretchers. Slowly, with the singing of Latin, German, and Old Church Slavonic hymns, the Christians started making their way out of Haram esh-Sharif.

But the procession was halted by a secretary sent by the emperor, accompanied by an officer with a platoon of Guards. The soldiers positioned themselves at the gate, and the secretary read from the stage: "This is what his divine majesty com-

---

18. "To these two deaths witness is borne here by Ernst Pauli."

mands: in order to bring the Christian people to their senses and protect them from evil-intentioned men who spread revolt and temptation, we consider it appropriate that the corpses of these two agitators killed by fire from heaven be displayed publicly on the Christian Road (Haret-en-Nasara), at the entrance to the main temple of this religion, called the church of the Holy Sepulcher, as well as of the Resurrection, so that all may become convinced that they are truly dead. Their obdurate sympathizers, who maliciously reject all our favors and insanely close their eyes to clear signs from the deity, will, by our mercy and our intercession before the heavenly father, be spared a richly deserved death by fire from heaven and will be left in complete freedom with the sole proviso (necessary for the common good) that they are forbidden to live in cities and other populous places, in order that they not confuse and tempt simpleminded, innocent people with their malicious inventions." After he had finished, the officer signaled and eight soldiers went up to the stretchers holding the bodies.

"Let that which is written be fulfilled," Professor Pauli said, and the Christians holding the stretchers silently surrendered them to the soldiers, who departed through the northwest gate, while the Christians, leaving through the northeast gate, hurriedly headed out of the city past the Mount of Olives toward Jericho on a road from which the police and two cavalry regiments had cleared the crowds. On the desert hills near Jericho the Christians decided to wait for several days. The next morning Christian pilgrims arrived from Jerusalem and reported what was happening in Zion.

After the court dinner all the council participants were invited into an enormous throne hall (near the traditional site of Solomon's throne); and the emperor, addressing the representatives of the Catholic hierarchy, announced to them that the good of the church obviously required from them the immediate election of a worthy successor to the apostle Peter. He further announced that, under the circumstances, the election process had to be streamlined, that his own presence as the leader and representative of the whole Christian world would more than make up for any omissions in ritual, and in the name of all Christians he proposed that the College of Cardinals elect his beloved friend and brother Apollonius, in order that their close relationship might cement and solidify the union of church and state for the common good of the two. The College of Cardinals retired to a special room for the conclave, and after an hour and a half they returned with the new pope, Apollonius.

While the election was being conducted, the emperor was meekly, sagely, and eloquently persuading the Orthodox and Evangelical representatives that, in view of the new great era of Christian history that had begun, they should end their old conflicts. He gave his word that Apollonius would know how to abolish forever all the historical abuses of papal power. Persuaded by this speech, the representatives of Orthodoxy and Protestantism composed an act of the unification of the churches, and when Apollonius entered the hall with the cardinals, to the joyful shouts of the whole assembly, the Greek archbishop and the Evangelical pastor brought to him their document. "Accipio et approbo et laetifacatur cor meum,"[19] said Apollonius, and he signed it. "I am as much a true Orthodox and a true Evangelist as I am a true Catholic," he added, and affably embraced the Greek and the German. He then went up to the emperor, who embraced him, holding him for a long time in his arms.

Meanwhile, peculiar points of light began to dart through the palace and temple in all directions, growing and changing

19. "I accept and approve and let my heart rejoice."

into the luminous forms of strange creatures, and flowers never before seen on earth sprinkled down from above, filling the air with an unfamiliar aroma. From above, the enchanting, soul-permeating, heart-rending sounds of musical instruments never heard before were wafting down, and the angelic voices of unseen singers were praising the new lords of heaven and earth. Meanwhile, a terrifying underground din erupted in the north-west corner of the Middle palace, beneath "kubbet-el-aruach," i.e., the "cupola of souls," the place, according to Islamic tradition, of the entrance to the underworld. When, on the emperor's invitation, the assembly moved in that direction, everyone clearly heard countless voices, thin and piercing—impossible to say whether of children or of demons—exclaiming: "The time has come. Release us, saviors, saviors!" But when Apollonius, falling down on the rock, thrice shouted downward something in an unknown language, the voices grew silent and the underground din stopped.

Meanwhile, an immense crowd surrounded Haram esh-Sharif. When night came, the emperor, together with the new pope, went out on the eastern terrace, eliciting a "storm of applause." He affably nodded in all directions, while Apollonius launched fireworks which he took from large bushels brought to him by cardinal-deacons; magnificent Roman candles, rockets, and fiery fountains, phosphorescently pearly or brightly irides-cent, continuously burst in the air, and before reaching the ground turned into countless multicolored sheets of paper with total and unconditional indulgences for all sins, past, present, and future. The rejoicing of the people transcended all bounds. True, some asserted that they had seen with their own eyes how the indulgences changed into disgusting toads and snakes. Nev-ertheless, the overwhelming majority were ecstatic, and the fes-tivities continued for several more days, with the new wonder-working pope performing tricks so unusual and improbable that it would be impossible to describe them.

Meanwhile, on the desert heights of Jericho, the Christians fasted and prayed. On the evening of the fourth day, after it had grown dark, Professor Pauli and nine companions made their way to Jerusalem, riding on donkeys and taking with them a cart; on side-streets leading past Haram esh-Sharif they arrived at Haret-en-Nasara and approached the entrance to the Church of the Resurrection, in front of which the bodies of Pope Peter and Elder John lay on the pavement. At this hour this street was deserted; the whole city had gone to Haram esh-Sharif. The sentries were sunk in a deep slumber. Those who came for the bodies found that they were not touched by the slightest decay and had not even undergone *rigor mortis*. They lifted the bodies onto stretchers and covered them with cloaks; they then returned to their friends by the same roundabout route. As soon as they lowered the stretchers onto the earth, the spirit of life entered the dead men. Peter and John stirred, trying to throw off the cloaks covering them. With joyful shouts everyone started to help them, and soon both men who had come back from the dead rose to their feet, healthy and unharmed.

Elder John, come back from the dead, spoke: "And so, my children, we have not been separated. This is what I say to you now: It is time to fulfill Christ's final prayer regarding his disciples, that they be one as he himself is one with the Father. For this unity of Christ, let us honor, my children, our beloved brother Peter. Let him henceforth shepherd Christ's lambs. Let it be so, brother!" And he embraced Peter. Professor Pauli approached them: "Tu est Petrus!" he addressed the pope. "Jetzt ist es gründlich erwiesen und ausser jedem Zweifel gesetzt."[20]

20. "This is now proved fundamentally and is not subject to any doubt."

And he firmly pressed Peter's hand with his own right hand and gave his left hand to Elder John with the words: "So also, Väterchen—nun sind wir ja Eins in Christo."[21] That is how the unification of the churches took place in the middle of a dark night in a high and solitary place. But the darkness of night was suddenly illuminated by a bright radiance, and a great sign appeared in heaven: a woman clothed with the sun, with the moon under her feet, and on her head a crown of twelve stars. This figure remained motionless for a time, and then she slowly moved southward. Pope Peter raised his staff and proclaimed: "That is our banner. Let us follow her." And he went in the direction of the vision, accompanied by both elders and the whole crowd of Christians—toward God's mountain, Sinai...

(*Here the reader stopped.*)

A LADY—Why did you stop?

MR. Z.—The manuscript breaks off there. Father Pansophius did not have time finish his tale. When he was already ill, he told me he wanted to write more—"when I recover." But he did not recover, and the end of his narrative is buried together with him in Danilov Monastery.

A LADY—But you must remember what he told you—so tell us.

MR. Z.—I only remember the general outline. After the spiritual leaders and representatives of Christianity had withdrawn into the Arabian desert, into which crowds of faithful zealots streamed to them from all lands, the new pope with his miracles and spectacles could unimpededly corrupt all the remaining Christians, the superficial ones who had not yet become disenchanted with the Antichrist. He announced that by the power of his keys he had opened the doors between this

---

21. "And so, dear fathers, henceforth we are one in Christ."

world and the next; intercourse between the living and the dead, and between humans and demons, did in fact become a common phenomenon, and new unheard-of types of mystical fornication and demonolatry arose.

But just when the emperor had begun to think he was on solid ground with regard to the religious problem and, in obedience to the insistent suggestions of the "father's" secret voice, proclaimed himself to be the one true incarnation of the supreme deity of the universe, a new calamity befell him, from a direction no one had expected: the Jews rebelled. This nation, whose numbers at that time had reached thirty million, had not been entirely averse to helping prepare and consolidate the superman's universal successes. When he moved his residence to Jerusalem, he secretly fueled rumors among the Jews that his main goal was to establish a universal kingdom of Israel, and the Jews therefore recognized him as the Messiah and offered him their boundless and ecstatic devotion. But suddenly they rebelled, in a frenzy of wrath and revenge. This turn of events, which unquestionably had been foretold both in the Bible and in tradition, was described by Father Pansophius perhaps a little too crudely and realistically. What happened was that the Jews, who had thought that the emperor was an Israelite by blood, discovered by chance that *he was not even circumcised*. That very day all Jerusalem, and the next day all Palestine, were engulfed by rebellion. A boundless and fervent devotion to the savior of Israel, the promised Messiah, was replaced by an equally boundless and fervent hatred for the lying deceiver, the brazen pretender.

All Jewry rose as if it were one man, and its enemies were amazed to see that in its deepest depths the soul of Israel lives not by the calculations and desires of Mammon but by the power of its heart's most cherished desire—by the hope and wrath of its age-old messianic faith. The emperor, not expecting such an explosion, lost his composure and issued a decree sentencing to death all disobedient Jews and Christians. Many thousands, and tens of thousands, having no time to arm themselves, were mercilessly massacred. But soon a million-man army of Jews took Jerusalem and trapped the Antichrist in Haram esh-Sharif. He was left only with some units of Guards, which were unable to overcome the foe's massive forces. The emperor was able to escape through the ranks of the invaders by means of his pope's magic, and he soon re-appeared in Syria with an immense army of gentiles from different nations. The Jews went out to meet him with little probability of success.

But the clash between the two armies had barely begun when an earthquake of unprecedented intensity occurred: beneath the Dead Sea, near which the imperial forces had assembled, the crater of an enormous volcano had opened, and flows of lava, creating a lake of fire, swallowed the emperor and his countless regiments, as well as pope Apollonius, all of whose magic could not help him. Meanwhile, the Jews fled to Jerusalem, in fear and trembling beseeching the God of Israel for salvation. The moment they saw the Holy City, the sky opened up with tremendous lightning spreading from east to west, and they saw Christ descending to them attired like a king and with wounds from the nails in his outstretched hands. At that time, a crowd of Christians was advancing from Sinai to Zion, led by Peter, John, and Paul, while from all directions other ecstatic crowds ran to meet them: these were the Jews and Christians who had been executed by the Antichrist. They had come back to life and were to reign with Christ for a thousand years.

That is how Father Pansophius wanted to end his tale, whose subject was not the world-ending catastrophe but only the resolution of our historical process consisting in the appearance, glorification, and destruction of the Antichrist.

At the Dawn
of Mist-Shrouded Youth

*With Selected Letters
to Ekaterina Romanova*

Translator's Introduction

COMPARE THE VISION of Julie in "At the Dawn of Mist-Shrouded Youth":

> When I regained consciousness, I saw only the bright sunlight, a strip of the blue sky, and in that light and in the midst of that sky, the face of a beautiful woman was bending down to me, and she was gazing at me with marvelous familiar eyes and whispering something quiet and gentle to me. . . . A rosy light was emanating from her face! . . . It was as if my entire being . . . had melted and become a single sweet, luminous, and passionless sensation; and in this sensation, as in a clear mirror, one miraculous image was fixedly reflected; and I felt and knew that this one image contained all.[1]

with Solovyov's vision of Sophia in the Egyptian desert:

> *. . . I heard a gentle whisper: "Sleep, my poor friend."*
> *Then I fell into a deep sleep; and when I waked*
> *The fragrance of roses wafted from earth and heaven.*
>
> *And in the purple of the heavenly glow*
> *You gazed with eyes full of an azure fire,*
> *And your gaze was like the first shining*
> *Of the universal and creative day.*

---

1. See p. 67 of the present volume.

What is, what was, and what will be were here
Embraced within that one fixed gaze... The seas
And rivers all turned blue beneath me, as did
The distant forest and the snow-capped mountain heights.

I saw it all, and all of it was one,
One image there of beauty feminine...
The immeasurable was confined within that image.
Before me, in me, you alone were there.[2]

In one case, the narrator regains consciousness; in the other he comes out of a deep sleep. In one case, he sees "a strip of the blue sky"; in the other, "the purple of the heavenly glow." In one case, "something quiet and gentle" is whispered to him; in the other, he hears a "gentle whisper." In one case, "a rosy light was emanating from her face"; in the other, her "eyes were full of azure fire." In one case, "one miraculous image was fixedly reflected; and I felt and knew that this one image" contained all"; in the other case, "I saw it all, and all of it was one, One image there of beauty feminine."

It is as if Solovyov is describing the same vision of Sophia, although the first occurred on a train to Kharkov in May 1872,[3] when Solovyov was nineteen years old, whereas the second occurred in the Egyptian desert in November 1875. It could be argued, of course, that Solovyov did not have either experience, that these visions of feminine radiance and universal oneness were literary fabrications—the first published some twenty

2. See Vladimir Solovyov's "Three Meetings," pp. 101–112 of the present volume.

3. S.M. Lukianov (see *Vl. S. Solovyov v ego molodye gody: Materialy k biografii*, Book I, Petrograd, 1916, pp 281–282) deduces that 22 May 1872 is the date this journey began.

years after the event in a semi-fictionalized memoir of his youth, the other twenty-three years after the event in a very peculiar poetical memoir. Or it could be argued that these are two literary reworkings of the same authentic primordial vision, the true character of which is now lost to the world.[4]

Let us accept, though, that we have a relatively accurate description (transformed in some way, but how we do not know) of two different events that actually took place. And if we accept this, we would have to acknowledge that Solovyov had four (not three) meetings with Sophia; and that, remarkably, in this fourth meeting (the second chronologically), Sophia, the Divine Radiance, found abode in a living woman. The center of the vision on the train is a woman's face, as it is in the vision at the British Museum:

> *... all around was filled with golden azure.*
> *And before me she was shining again—*
> *But only her face, it was her face alone.*[5]

Could it be that Solovyov had met a living woman in the Museum, and could, she, like Julie, have been transformed into an abode for Sophia? And is it common for women to become her abode? Do they need a special gift, or is the transformation inspired by a special sensitivity of the visionary?

There are other doubts and questions: Did Solovyov and Julie have sexual intercourse on the train?[6] Did this mean the end of Solovyov's virginity? And did the erotic episode somehow trigger the sophianic vision? Mochulsky and others have

---

4. Another similarity between "At the Dawn of Mist-Shrouded Youth" and "Three Meetings" is that both display comical elements.

5. See p. 106 of the present volume.

6. See suspension points, p. 63 of the present volume.

pointed out that Solovyov's other visions of Sophia were triggered by infatuations: the first vision, in the Church, when Solovyov was nine, by an infatuation with a girl of nine; the visions in the British Museum and in the Egyptian desert by Solovyov's relationship with E. M. Polivanova. If there was such a close connection between the erotic and the sophianic in Solovyov's life, might it not be the case that Solovyov's visions were actually pseudo-sophianic or even antisophianic? Could these visions have been spiritual deceptions or illusions (*prelest'*)? Is Solovyov guilty of confusing the celestial Aphrodite with the earthly Aphrodite? (And indeed, even his use of the same name, Aphrodite, for the two entities is suspicious.)

In my opinion, these visions are truly sophianic: the erotic is expelled before the sophianic encounter is enacted. (The word "passionless" in the above-quoted passage from "At the Dawn of Mist-Shrouded Youth" serves to support this.) Sophia is virginal: her medium is *sophrosyne*, integral wisdom or virginity (Russ. *tselomudrie*). Even those who have lost their virginity (or half-lost it, like Solovyov, by playing with the fire of the feminine erotic element) can encounter her if she desires it and permits it.

❧❧❧

Ekaterina Romanova is the young cousin whom Solovyov loved at the time of the events described in "At the Dawn of Mist-Shrouded Youth": she is the Olga of the story. Solovyov was journeying to see her in Kharkov, perhaps to propose marriage, when the encounter on the train fatally altered his plans. Ekaterina was the last of Solovyov's "kissing cousins," girls with whom he had pre-erotic experiences dating to his early teenage years. These cousins can be considered the garden where his erotic life was nurtured and grew.

One has the sense that the beautiful Ekaterina is important chiefly as a foil for the luminous Julie (always remembering, though, that "At the Dawn of Mist-Shrouded Youth" is not, strictly speaking, a memoir: we do not know to what extent the events described actually happened).

The letters are marked by an absence of the sophianic: Ekaterina is no Julie. The letters are humdrum, and therein lies their importance: they are the most important documentary evidence we have concerning the evolution of Solovyov's consciousness at the crucial age of nineteen or twenty. They give us an idea of his intellectual preoccupations, especially of his Schopenhauerean pessimism: "Joy and pleasure in this life are dangerous, for they are illusory; unhappiness and sorrow are often the only salvation."[7] They show how Solovyov liked to pontificate and to lecture young girls on such subjects as religious faith and the search for the path one should follow in life. They develop his view "that the entire grand evolution of Western philosophy and science…has…worked out a new, worthy form for Christianity."[8] They provide a glimpse of his erotic life where it does not border on the sophianic element. Ekaterina is an object of ordinary love for Solovyov; Julie is an object of "adoration,"[9] as befits an incarnation of the Divine Sophia.

❧

In his Author's Note to "Three Meetings," Solovyov called the vision in the Egyptian desert "the most significant thing that

7. See p. 72 of the present work. This world view is also, somewhat comically, reflected in "At the Dawn of Mist-Shrouded Youth": in Solovyov's preaching of "the self-negation of the will."
8. See p. 93 of the present volume.
9. After the sophianic moment, Solovyov notes that Julie "silently and serenely bore my adoration" (see p. 67 of the present volume).

had ever happened in my life." I submit that the encounter with Julie (the "fourth meeting") is the second most significant thing that had happened in his life.

✦

"At The Dawn of Mist-Shrouded Youth" (*Na zare tumannoi iunosti*) was first published in the journal *Russkaya Mysl'*, May 1892. Solovyov's letters to Ekaterina Romanova were first published in *Pis'ma Vladimira Sergeevicha Solovyova*, ed. E. L. Radlov, vol. III (St. Petersburg: Obshchestvennaia pol'za, 1911) pp. 56–106. The present selection represents the first translation into English of any substantial block of Solovyov's letters. It follows Radlov's enumeration scheme. The dates are, of course, all given in the old style. A number of letters deemed by the editor to be of minor importance are omitted, and some letters have been abridged, with omissions indicated by [...]. Some minor postscripts have also been omitted. A number of Solovyov's letters to Romanova after 1873 have been lost; Lukianov considered them not to be crucial, since they were written after the termination of the love affair, and do not have the drama of the original letters.[10]

This translation first appeared in *At the Dawn of Mist-Shrouded Youth With Selected Letters to Ekaterina Romanova* by Vladimir Solovyov, Variable Press, 1999, and has been slightly revised for the present edition. The reader is invited to compare "At The Dawn of Mist-Shrouded Youth" with Solovyov's great sophianic poem "Three Meetings," also reprinted in the present edition.

BORIS JAKIM
Revised, October 2014

---

10. Lukianov, op. cit., p. 274.

At the Dawn
of Mist-Shrouded Youth
(*A Story*)

THIS PAST NIGHT I did not sleep at all. At such times my sick
fantasy usually evokes incoherent shadows of scenes and events,
both real and imagined, in combinations both varied and unexpected. But this time my insomnia's delirium was coherent and
unified. Arising before me with ever increasing clarity came a
continuous stream of details related to a certain event that was
part of the deep past and that had been completely forgotten—
or so I thought. And though this event had begun in a totally
insignificant way, its conclusion left a profound mark on my
inner life. I am happy that my infirm memory has brought back
to me all these details; and I hasten to record them while they
are still fresh.

I

I was then nineteen years old. This event had taken place at the
end of May; I had just moved on to the final course at the University, and was traveling by train from Moscow to Kharkov,
where I was to have an extremely important conversation with
my cousin Olga,[1] for whom I had long—for three or four
months—been nurturing a tender and highly elevated love. It
was because of her that I had decided to make a large detour,

---

1. Olga is certainly Ekaterina Romanova. See "Letters to Ekaterina
Romanova," p. 71 of the present volume.

SOPHIA, GOD & A SHORT TALE ABOUT THE ANTICHRIST

since the real destination of my journey was the Kirghiz steppe, where I intended to take a fermented-milk cure as a treatment for my constitution, so shaken by my immoderate consumption of German books.

I took my seat in second class. A young blonde wearing a light-gray traveling dress sat down opposite me in the other compartment of the car. She was speaking gaily and affectionately with three men who were accompanying her. When the train got under way, she kept nodding to them out the window and waving with her handkerchief.

The divider separating the two compartments of the car was quite low, and above it I had an unobstructed view of my *vis-à-vis*. And so, I occupied myself with observing her, since there was nothing more interesting to do in the car. She was short, rather thin, and with a fine figure. Her face, with its irregular nose and wide mouth, was far from beautiful. But when she gazed tenderly with her bright eyes, her simple face, not at all beautiful, grew highly appealing. It was not that her gaze was particularly expressive; but it possessed something more profound than thought—a kind of serene light without fire or flash. It was her eyes that attracted and intrigued me at first sight. I also noticed her lovely thick hair. It seemed to me that she, too, would often gaze at me with an approving smile, whereupon I, naturally, would put on an abstracted and disillusioned air. But I could not bring myself to talk to her, partly because it was inconvenient to do so over the divider, but even more so because, despite my proud demeanor, I was extremely timid, and the gaze of any woman was capable of making my heart sink and rendering my tongue mute.

She was visited at several intervals by a passenger from another car—an older woman. I learned later that this woman, traveling with her family in first class, was a relative of my blonde companion's husband. They conversed, often in French, about everyday practical matters. The only thing I learned from their conversation was that they were Muscovites and that they were traveling to the Crimea.

II

There was no question I liked this woman in the gray dress. She turned her head so subtly and exquisitely as she spoke; all her movements were so gracious and feminine.

"Nevertheless, my Olga is much prettier," I told myself. And closing my eyes, I began to think about Olga and my imminent meeting with her in Kharkov, a meeting she was not expecting. I imagined how she would cry out when she saw me; how she would grow pale—perhaps even faint—from the unexpected joy; how I would then revive her and what I would tell her.

But do not think I was expecting an ordinary amorous encounter with nothing but caresses and tendernesses. O no! I was very far from such thoughtlessness. Of course, I admitted an element of tenderness, but it could only be the background of the picture—the essence was to be elsewhere. I wished to see Olga so as to "anchor our relationship in a foundation of the self-negation of the will." And that was truly my intent. And what I wanted to say to her was something like this:

"My dearest Olga, I love you and am glad that you love me too. But I know, and you must learn to understand, that all of life—and consequently the flower of life, love—is only a phantom and a deception. We madly aspire to happiness, but in reality we find only suffering. Our will eternally deceives us, forcing us to chase blindly after intrinsically worthless objects as if they were supremely good and blissful. Our will is the first and greatest evil from which we must emancipate ourselves. To accomplish this, we must reject all of the will's suggestions, suppress all our personal aspirations, renounce all our desires and hopes. If you are capable of understanding me (and I am certain that you are), then we can follow life's path together. But know that, with me, you will never find so-called family happiness, a happiness invented by dull-witted philistines. I have learned what the truth is, and my goal is to actualize it for others: to expose and destroy the universal deception. You understand that such a task has nothing in common with pleasure. I can promise you only hard struggle and suffering side by side."

This is what I intended to tell the pretty seventeen year old Olga. Generally speaking, the doctrine of the total worthlessness of all that exists constituted the main theme of my conversations with my female cousins—of whom I had several and with whom I successively fell in love. Of course, I was in part acquainted with the evil and insignificance of life from my own personal experience as well. I knew from my experience that my cousins' kisses were not things of eternal significance and that an extra glass of wine causes headaches. But even if my life-experience was not yet sufficiently rich, I had read much and thought even more; and by the age of eighteen my thinking had brought me to the firm conviction that the entirety of temporal life, since it consisted exclusively of evils and sufferings, must be destroyed completely as quickly as possible. I had reached this conclusion with my own mind, but it did not take me long to become convinced that I was not alone in having such an opinion: it had been elaborated in very great detail by certain famous German philosophers. However, at that time I was, in part, a Slavophile; and therefore, although I accepted that the Germans could abolish the universe in theory, I was convinced that the practical realization of this task fell exclusively on the Russian nation. Moreover, I did not doubt in my soul that I would be the one to give the first signal for the world's destruction.

III

But self-negation of the will and the necessity of destroying the universe were not the most abstruse elements of the doctrine that I had been teaching my fortunate cousins. A year before my journey to Kharkov, one of my cousins—the blue-eyed but fiery Liza, who was then the object of my passion—was, one fine summer evening, found worthy of being initiated into the mysteries of *transcendental idealism.*

Strolling with her through a neglected country park, I explained to her—not without passion although sometimes unsure of the terms I used to convey my thoughts—that space, time, and causality are merely the subjective forms of our cognition and that the whole world, which exists in these forms, is only our representation, that is, that it, essentially, does not exist at all. When I arrived at this conclusion, my cousin, who all the while had been looking at me very seriously with her large greenish eyes, smiled and remarked wickedly:

"But why is it that yesterday you kept talking about the Last Judgment?"

"About what Last Judgment?"

"Oh you know, about the fact that everything must be destroyed. If in your opinion the world doesn't exist, why then are you so anxious to destroy it?"

This contradiction embarrassed me only for an instant.

"When you are oppressed by a frightening nightmare, don't you want to free yourself of it?" I answered triumphantly.

Suddenly, for no apparent reason, she gave out a peal of laughter.

"What is it?" I asked with displeasure.

"Just think," she said, laughing and firmly pressing my hand. "Just think, last night I dreamt that my James (her Irish setter) was not a dog at all but the commander of a Byelorussian Hussars regiment, and that all our officers had to show him proper respect, but instead of 'respected sir', they all had to address him as '*flea*spected sir'."

She completed this unexpected news with a kiss that was just as unexpected, and suddenly ran away, crying out to me from a distance:

"Let's go gather the strawberries. I saw there are many ripe ones."

And I went to gather the strawberries, although the categorical imperative, which philistines call conscience, was quite clearly hinting to me that, on my part, this was not the self-negation but—just the opposite—the self-assertion of the will.

But so sweetly did the merry Liza incline her little blonde head over the strawberries, so coquettishly did she lift her dress up above her ankles, the silver clasps of her shoes sparkling in the sunlight, that I had no desire at all to free myself of this pleasant nightmare; the book in my room with its unread chapter on *the synthetic unity of transcendental apperception* would have to wait.

And when, sitting on the train on my way to Kharkov, for some reason I remembered this small episode, a dim foreboding of future falls into sin stirred in my soul.

IV

Meanwhile, evening was fast approaching. The train had stopped at a small station. We heard the merry and impatient ringing of a little bell: a troika had arrived for the purpose, it would seem, of picking up a gray-haired gentleman and two young ladies who had descended onto the platform with their things and were animatedly conversing with the station manager.

I stuck my head out the window. A strong fragrance of lilac wafted from the dense garden adjacent to the station house. Little peasant girls were selling bouquets of lilies of the valley. There was a ringing sound some distance away. Someone was playing the piano in a small outbuilding, while a company of local residents of both sexes sat sipping tea and merrily conversing in a corner of the garden.

The woman in the gray dress strolled about the platform and smiled sweetly at me. I gazed at her with the same serene pleasure as at everything else. My soul was peaceful and content this evening. The evil and suffering of existence had retreated so deeply into the very essence of things that I did not feel their presence at all—but this might have been because at this moment I did not desire anything, and in everything that surrounded me I saw merely a landscape.

And when the train departed, it was with the same peaceful pleasure, not thinking about anything and not desiring anything, that I gazed at the dense birch grove that with a welcoming whisper greeted our train and embraced it from both sides, that beckoned to us with a promise of repose, and that smiled meekly, its treetops gilded with the evening rays.

But this peace of the soul was disrupted in the most unexpected manner. When we arrived at Tula and no other passengers were left in our car aside from the woman in the gray dress and me, suddenly, with much shouting and brouhaha, a crowd of new travelers entered. This was a troupe of French actors going to Orel—though quite possibly they were not actors but merely acrobats. There were seven or eight of them, both men and women. The men were pretty drunk and their behavior was rather unseemly. At first they wanted to play cards, but couldn't find any. Then, taking off their coats, they started doing gymnastics: hanging on the crossbeams, swinging back and forth, turning somersaults; and two of them even tried leapfrogging each other, though without success.

The behavior of the women was just as unseemly. With loud laughter and cries they engaged in jesting quarrels with the men. One of the women, a rather attractive one, took off a shoe and threw it at one of the gymnasts, who, in revenge, grabbed her by the foot and tried to drag her onto the floor, but instead fell flat on the floor with a thud, provoking indescribable glee among the whole troupe.

V

The woman in the gray dress had been observing this performance with a certain degree of curiosity. But she was evidently scandalized by the last episode. She got up and went over to me (I was sitting at the edge of the couch near the aisle).

"Can I hide behind you from this company? They are so horrid."

I bowed.

She sat down next to me, by the window.

My soul rejoiced that my sweet companion had taken the first step so simply and easily; and all my timidity disappeared completely. After a few minutes we were conversing like old friends.

It turned out that I knew her husband by name. They had young children.

"Ah! How difficult it is to educate children when you yourself are lacking in education. I thought about this for a long time

and decided to leave them to fate—let them grow and be educated as they know best. At least I won't be spoiling anything."

With the serious air of a mentor, as befitted a nineteen-year-
old philosopher, I remarked that there was still time for her to
undertake her own education.

"Ah! You have no idea what you're saying. I'm so lazy. I
have no character at all, not a drop! And then where is an education to be found? Some people advise one thing, others something else. No, it would better if I remained as I am!"

My companion's education had in fact been limited to
exquisite manners and a knowledge of French.

"Sometimes, however, I do read the Moscow Gazette as
well as novels, only not the serious kind... But you probably
wish to become a scholar? Ah, please don't! That's so hideous!
That's almost the same as becoming an acrobat like these char-
acters: it's every bit as unnatural but much more boring. And
then it's so harmful to one's health. Even now you're so thin
and pale. That's a pity. You know what: Come to visit us in the
Crimea. You need to bathe in the sea—that fortifies the constitution... And how merry it is there! A large crowd. Nobody
does anything, and everyone's happy. And the air there is special. This will be my fourth summer there, and every time I'm
there, I fall in love... And just imagine: it's always recipro-
cated," she added, evidently genuinely surprised by this cir-
cumstance.

"You think I'm lying because I'm so unattractive? But I
assure you it's true. I must say, though, that everyone falls in
love with everyone there. Some get married: every year there's
a wedding. And some fall in love without getting married... My
God, I keep talking nonsense! Whatever must you think of me!"

I hastened to remark that, although love is an evil and
deception, illegitimate love is, in any case, much more pardon-

able than legalized love. That was my sincere belief at the time. Marriage, especially happy marriage, filled me, an extreme pessimist, with indignation to the depths of my soul; for it was this institution that was the chief support of this whole world whose destruction was the supreme goal of my aspirations.

My companion clearly did not understand what I was trying to say.

"My sorrow lies in the fact," she said, "that, for some reason, a great many men fall in love with me, and I find it horribly difficult to offend or cause pain to anyone, least of all to those who love me. The most horrible thing for me is to refuse anyone anything. I would like to love everyone and give everyone pleasure. But that's totally impossible here. Here everything's arranged so horridly: everyone is jealous, envious, of everyone else; everyone interferes with everyone else. If you fall in love with someone so as not to cause him pain, then you offend someone else. It's just awful! And then I have a husband and children. I've decided never to deceive my husband—and to tell the truth he does not demand much from me. But there are such strange people that they have no desire to understand anything, and they demand the impossible as though they were little children... Ah, sometimes I want to die! Only not now. Now I'm in high spirits. I'm so glad I've made your acquaintance."

She fell silent for a moment.

"You know, I sometimes think of the afterlife, and I imagine that there things will be just the opposite: nobody will interfere with anybody else. And it will be possible to love everyone, everyone. And nobody will be offended by that... Ah, how stupid I am. I don't know how to express myself, but, there's no doubt, I understand how it will be."

She pressed her hands to her head and grew pensive.

VI

It was already quite dark. It had grown quiet in the train car. The French actors were worn out by their antics and were lying down to sleep here and there as best they could. From time to time one heard incoherent sounds, someone muttering in his sleep.

"You're probably not going to sleep?" my companion suddenly asked.

I nodded.

"Nor am I. Let's talk. Only let me make myself more comfortable."

She took off her hat and let down her hair.

In the sublunary sphere there are objects that, from my early childhood, have had an irresistible effect upon me. And during the epoch of my life that I am now remembering, the sight of such magical objects would rob my pessimism of all its strength and make my ascetic morality lower its wings with shameful obedience. Among such objects were a woman's long hair spread out over her shoulders. And I had never yet seen such luxuriant hair as that which was now present before my eyes. And the longer I looked at it, the further and further the distinction between eternal essence and transient phenomenon receded from my mental gaze, and the lower and lower drooped the wings of my self-negating will.

I took a thick lock of this radiant, fragrant hair and brought it up to my lips.

A quiet smile and silence.

She lowered her hands to her knees and inclined her head. In this pose with her hair down she was quite attractive. I wanted to tell her this, to tell her that I loved her, but the words would not leave my tongue. Instead, I bent down to her lowered hands and began to cover them with kisses.

"How strange you are! Who gave you permission to do that?"

I lifted my head, whispering a naive apology for my impulse; and suddenly I felt a long, soundless, hot kiss on my lips.

. . . .

The next morning I was somber and morose. The distinction between good and evil, which I did not remember even once during the past night, now presented itself to my mind with total clarity and distinctness.

How shameful! I, a pessimist and ascetic, implacable foe of the earthly principle, had surrendered to this principle without a struggle, without the slightest attempt at resistance, worse— with a kind of joyous readiness and anticipation; I had at once recognized the authority of this principle and delighted in my enslavement to it. I, who virtually from my cradle had recognized the vanity of desire, the deceitfulness of happiness, the illusoriness of pleasures; I, who had labored for three years to fortify this truth innate in me with unassailable walls of transcendental philosophy, I was now seeking and could find—at least for a moment—bliss in the embrace of a woman with whom I was barely acquainted but who was obviously shallow and totally uneducated.

> Toward what, unhappy one, have I been striving!
> Before whom have I lowered my proud mind!
> Who was it that I shamefully adored
> With the rapture of pure thoughts!

Never had I been subjected to such humiliation. Of course, in the past I had often had occasion to kiss my cousins. But this was completely different. In the first place, the thing was not in the kisses themselves but in their intensity as well as in their extensiveness. Secondly, my cousins were more or less adepts of my doctrine; and I could consider these kisses as an external expression of inner spiritual relations. But in my new acquaintance I could see absolutely no capacity for higher philosophical understanding. Furthermore, for her I could betray my Olga, the Olga who had been so saddened by her separation from me, who understood me so well, and was to follow hand in hand with me the arduous path of the self-negation of the will.

I felt truly awful. Our ancestor Adam must have felt something akin to this on that sad day when, in exchange for his lost bliss, he was supplied with "coats of skins."[2]

VII

Julie (that is what my companion wanted me to call her) also was not very happy. She was not well. Evidently, she suffered from a rapid heart beat. She would frequently close her eyes and press a hand to her chest. With her mouth clamped shut in pain, with her closed eyes, and the unhealthy pallor of her face, she became quite unattractive. I was angry with her. I blamed her for everything. It was because of her, after all, that I had turned out to be trash, a mere rag. It was because of her that I had betrayed my principles, that I had brought shame upon myself. At that time I did not believe in the devil. So, Julie was to blame. Alas, in this respect too, I entirely resembled the old Adam, who, having sinned, tried to shift the blame to his weaker companion.

But my poor Eve, whenever her pains abated, would, as

---

2. Genesis 3:21.

before, start conversing sweetly with me. This irritated me even more. I was ready to hate her. Despite her extreme lack of education, she evidently liked to discuss lofty subjects. Everything that she said now seemed either absurd or trivial to me.

Among other things, she touched upon the emancipation of women. I rudely interrupted her:

"It seems to me that, even as it is, our women are too emancipated. If there's anything they're lacking, it wouldn't be freedom, of course, but rather restraint."

The hint was clear. Julie blushed slightly and raised her large eyes at me. There was nothing but sad surprise in her gaze. After a moment she again started speaking with me with the same sweetness.

I felt a stab in my heart. I was ashamed that I had offended her; but I utterly failed to appreciate the meekness with which she bore this offense. I did not like her. In order to make up for my rudeness, I forced myself to be nice to her, but my "niceness" was very cold and Julie noticed the insincerity of my tender declarations. Her gaze was sad, and she smiled sadly.

In Kursk we had to change trains. Julie had a reservation for a first-class compartment, whereas I bought a ticket for the second class. And so, we were separated. I pretended to be upset, but in my soul I was pleased. Her nearness had been burdensome; furthermore, as I got closer to Kharkov, my obligations with regard to Olga, the girl who truly understood me, appeared clearer and clearer to me.

Having accompanied Julie to her compartment, I sat down in my new place with lighter heart and in a good mood, and soon became acquainted with my fellow passengers. These were: a medical student from Kiev University; a young merchant from Taganrog in a cloth coat and a new black cap; and a man of indeterminate profession and age, dark-haired and with a dark-blue chin—a rich moneylender, as it turned out, also from Taganrog.

I got to talking with the young medical student. He was a provincial nihilist of the most extreme type. He at once recognized me as one of his own kind—"by the intelligent expression of your face," as he later explained to me, and also, perhaps, by my long hair and casual dress.

We opened our souls to each other. We were in complete agreement that the existing order of things must be destroyed as quickly as possible. But he thought that this destruction would be followed by the appearance of an earthly paradise, where poor, stupid, and vicious people would not exist, and all mankind would equitably enjoy all possible physical and intellectual goods in numberless phalansteries that would cover the globe; whereas I argued with animation that his view was not sufficiently radical, that, in actuality, not only the earth but even the whole universe must be radically destroyed, that if there were to be any life after this, it would be a totally different life, a purely transcendent life with no resemblance to the present one. He was a naturalistic radical, whereas I was a metaphysical radical.

We spoke and argued very fervently and loudly. Once the medical student tried to ask our fellow passengers for their opinion, but the moneylender with the blue chin only smiled apologetically and shrugged, while the young merchant muttered something totally unencouraging...something like "damned troublemakers," and turned his back to us.

At the conclusion of our dispute my opponent remarked that our theoretical positions might diverge but, since we had the same proximate practical goals and were both "honest radicals," we could be friends and allies; and we shook hands with feeling.

VIII

At that moment the door to our car opened, and Julie entered. She had come to invite me to join her in first class; she was the only one in her compartment, and being alone made her bored. She said we could travel together all the way to Kharkov.

I readily accepted her invitation, though in my soul I was unhappy. At that moment my new friend and ally interested me much more than she did. "Why is she compromising herself in this way? How stupid all this is!" I thought.

Exhaustion from the long journey, the unusual agitations of the sleepless night, finally, the intense, fervent conversation about abstruse abstractions—all this taken together must have completely unsettled my nerves. Julie and I left to go to her car. Preceding her, I was about to step out onto the second of the two iron connecting boards between the cars when I suddenly lost consciousness. I came to on the platform of my car. My new friend, who had seen us through the open door of the car and hastened to my assistance, later told me that I would certainly have fallen into the space between the cars and been crushed by the train that was going at full steam, if this "fine lady" had not grabbed me by the shoulders and held me on the platform.

I learned this later. When I regained consciousness, I saw only the bright sunlight, a strip of the blue sky, and in that light and in the midst of that sky, the face of a beautiful woman was bending down to me, and she was gazing at me with marvelous familiar eyes and whispering something quiet and gentle to me.

There is no doubt that this was Julie and that those were her eyes, but how everything else had changed! A rosy light was emanating from her face! How tall and magnificent she was! Something miraculous had happened within me. It was as if my entire being with all its thoughts, feelings, and desires had melted away and become a single infinite sweet, luminous, and passionless sensation; and in this sensation, as in a clear mirror, one miraculous image was fixedly reflected; and I felt and knew that this one image contained all. I loved with a new, all-engulfing, and infinite love; and in this love I felt the whole fullness and meaning of life for the first time.

With great care she led me to my former place. My friend, the medical student, courteously let her have the seat next to mine. At the next stop of the train, she led me to her compartment.

We were alone. I could not speak for a long time. All I could do was look at her with insane eyes and kiss the hem of her dress, her feet. She also did not say anything but only kept applying a handkerchief moistened with eau de cologne to my head. Finally, in an incoherent, fragmentary whisper I started conveying to her what was happening to me, how I loved her, that she meant everything to me, that this love had regenerated me, that this was a wholly other, new love, in which I was wholly forgetting myself, that only now had I understood that God exists in man, that goodness and true joy exist in life, that life's goal is not cold, dead negation...

She listened with clear eyes and happy smile. The revolutionary change that had occurred in me made her happy but, evidently, did not surprise her. She did not ask me about anything. Just as earlier she had silently and serenely borne my insults, so now she silently and serenely bore my adoration.

When I more or less came back to normal, she began to speak simply and calmly. For her it was love at first sight; and she was happy that I loved her now with so fine a love. She was certain that between the two of us there could be truly good relations. We must meet in Moscow. She would introduce me to her husband.

"But it would be better if you didn't come to the Crimea. I can't really trust myself. I'll be afraid for myself, and for you."

I said that I would do whatever she wanted.

We did not notice how the day ended, how the evening passed, and the moment of separation arrived. At the Kharkov station I remained with her until the last bell. As the train was leaving, she leaned out the window and extended both hands to me. The night was dark; no one paid us any attention—except perhaps some sentimental little star that had pity on me, noticing from above the abundant hot tears that flowed from my eyes onto those dear gentle hands.

The train had long disappeared from sight, but I kept standing at the same place.

IX

"What has happened, my friend? Have you washed yourself with salt water and thus turned into a pillar of salt? Don't grieve: it's not as though you have parted forever; you'll see each other again. I approve your taste: quite a honey, by George! Another time I might have fallen for her myself. Well let's go, señor!"

I silently followed the honest radical, and we took a carriage to Hotel Dagmar.

My soul was full of Julie until I fell asleep. But the next day the whole encounter seemed utterly fantastic to me in some sense and terribly distant. I had indeed experienced something; somewhere in the deepest corner of my soul, I felt something new, unprecedented. But that something had not yet merged with my real life. I knew that the past had to continue and take its course, as if nothing had happened. But what had in fact happened? It was subjective exaltation and nothing more!

I went to see Olga. Naturally, our meeting did not go at all as I had imagined it. To begin with, she wasn't home, which didn't fit into my plans. I departed, having left a note. Thus, when I arrived for the second time, she had already been forewarned about my presence in Kharkov—there was no longer sufficient ground for fainting and other extraordinary phenomena. She had just come back from a stroll outside the city. I found her greatly changed. She bore no resemblance to that gentle, semi-ethereal girl who had remained in my memory from our last meeting in the country: I had retained a vision of her coming out of the bathhouse wearing a light-blue cotton dress and with a dark braid carelessly slung over her back. Instead, I now encountered a completely grown-up and smartly attired young lady with familiar manners. She looked at me quite boldly and intently, her black eyes slightly reddened from sun and wind. There was something decisive and independent about her.

After the first brief questions about her family, her health, and so on, I got to the matter at hand. In her letters she wrote that she loved me—and now I had to explain to her my view of our relationship. I spoke briefly and unpersuasively. I felt that I was repeating some memorized lesson; every word resounded in my ears as something foreign and totally uninteresting. To tell the truth, my words were totally wooden.

Leaning her elbows on the table, she listened pensively. When I had finished my speech with its inevitable invitation to follow the path of the self-negation of the will with me, for the longest time she kept looking off into the distance, her eyes immobile; then she suddenly lowered her arms, raised her head, and, intently gazing at me, pronounced in a calm and firm voice:

"I do not wish to deceive you. I have been mistaken in my feelings. You're too smart and idealistic for me, and I don't love you enough to share your views and to unite my life with yours forever. You reject all pleasure, but pleasure is the only thing I understand. I will always love you like a relative. Let us be friends."

Let me hasten to note that this was my last attempt to convert young ladies to the path of the self-negation of the will. That same evening I left Kharkov, without even saying farewell to my new friend, the radical.

Four years later I met Julie in Italy, on the Riviera. But that was a meeting that can only be related on Christmas Eve.[3]

3. In the spring of 1876, after his experience in the Egyptian desert, Solovyov traveled to Italy, where he met Madame Nadezhda Evgeneevna Auer, who helped nurse him after he had injured his leg in a fall. In the 1890s, he dedicated two poems to her. Lukianov (see *Vl. S. Solovyov v ego molodye gody*: Book II, Petrograd, 1918, pp. 345–346) speculates that it was N. E. Auer whom Solovyov had in mind when he wrote that he had met Julie in Italy. However, we do not know if Julie and N. E. Auer were one and the same person, or if they were different women in whom Solovyov saw the same erotic and/or sophianic qualities.

Selected Letters to Ekaterina Romanova

1.

Moscow. 12 October 1871.

[...] You write, my friend, that you wish to spend more time at your studies this winter. But, please, do not pursue studies that are overly strenuous (here I return your advice to me), and for God's sake, don't study the natural sciences: in and of itself, this discipline is totally vacuous and illusory. Only *human* nature and human life are intrinsically worthy of study; and they can be best known from authentic works of poetry. Therefore, I advise you to read the great poets as much as this is possible for you. As a means to this, start studying English and improve your knowledge of German. Given your diligence, you will master them in no time.

This spring, if it is at all possible, I shall try to visit you in Kiev.

Farewell, my dear! Kisses to you, to my aunt, and to Poliksena.[1]

Write to me, please, and don't forget my address.

Vl. Solovyov.

P.S. Why is it you do not write about your Mama's health?

---

1. The aunt is Ekaterina Romanova's mother, A.S. Sheviakova, who was in poor health, and died on 18 January 1872, when Ekaterina was 16 years old. Poliksena was Ekaterina's sister.

2.

Moscow. 21 December 1871.

I cannot express, my dear friend Katya, what a benevolent effect your sweet concern has upon me; I shall try to be at least a little worthy of it. I become ashamed of myself when I think that you are consoling and encouraging me even though your life is a thousand times more difficult than mine: Without even mentioning your mother's illness, I know that there is nothing worse than this constant bondage to the external, petty life for someone like you who strives for something else, something better. But I am comforted by the firm certainty that you have another—inner—life inaccessible to any petty externalities. Whatever may be your external situation, you will always preserve your inner moral strength, which makes you free and which nothing external can take away from you. Perhaps it is even a good thing that this external life has turned out to be so devoid of comfort for you: for this life is fully governed by the wise saying: *the worse things are, the better they are.* Joy and pleasure in this life are dangerous, for they are illusory; unhappiness and sorrow are often the only salvation. People have known this for almost two thousand years, but they do not stop chasing happiness like little children. Let at least you and I, my dear, stop being little children in this respect.—Write to me, my friend, about everything you are thinking and feeling; and be certain of my sincere, heartfelt sympathy. You are greatly mistaken if you think that I am entirely immersed in my *folly*, as you absolutely accurately describe my stupid romance. For a long time this folly has stopped interfering with any of my activities, and now it is almost over—except for infrequent remembrances of it during sleepless nights.

Vsevolod[2] truly seems to think you're a little girl: the books

---

2. Solovyov's older brother, the future novelist.

about which you write do not require any special preparation, and are by no means "too serious." On the contrary, strictly speaking, they are not serious enough. Nevertheless, I think they can bring some benefit; and so, if you have a chance, read them. But never be governed by the authority of books: let that be your general rule. Therefore, if you read something that is even strictly proven, but your inner conviction does not agree with it, then believe yourself more than any book—because, in serious questions, unprovable and unconscious conviction is the voice of God.

Farewell, my dear, my darling. A firm embrace from

Your friend forever,

Vl. Solovyov

P.S. My deepest thanks for the picture. As soon as I have one taken of myself, I shall send it.

3.

27 January 1872.

I have thought much about you, my dear Katya, with reference to your last letter. For the time being I will not say anything about your understanding of the second path that you have decided to follow. The meaning you attribute to it now— is not important. What is important is the fact that you have rejected the first path, the ordinary one; that is, the fact that you have rejected what constitutes the whole of life for the majority of people: the life of egotism, personal interests, with a stupid phantom of happiness as the final goal. You have understood that this is falsehood and evil, that this life is death. And not only have you understood this; you have also made the firm decision to emancipate yourself from this falsehood and evil. With this decision, you have already taken the first, most difficult and important step toward such emancipation. But there is still much to do in the future.

If that which is considered real life is false, then there must be another life, the true one. The embryo of this *true* life is within us ourselves, because if this embryo did not exist, we would be satisfied with the falsehood surrounding us and not seek anything better. If we constantly dwelled in total darkness and knew nothing about the light, we would then not complain about the darkness and not seek the light. True life does exist within us, but it is suppressed or distorted by our limited personhood, by our egotism. It is necessary to know this true life as it is in itself, in its purity; and to know the means by which it can be attained. All this was revealed long ago to humanity by true Christianity, but, historically, Christianity itself has experienced the influence of that false life, that evil which it should have destroyed. And this falsehood so obscured Christianity that, at the present time, it is as difficult to understand the truth in Christianity as it is to arrive directly at the truth by oneself.

But one who has firmly renounced falsehood will certainly arrive at truth. You have taken this first difficult step, and I am fully certain that you yourself will attain the goal—although...[3] you will have to wade through a lot of garbage. But the other path too is not strewn with roses—everywhere there is only suffering. The difference is that, on the true path, the suffering redeems us and leads to truth, whereas the suffering of false life is sterile and meaningless.

Farewell, my dear. With true love your

Vl. Solovyov.

---

3. Three lines are crossed out in the original at this point.

4.

Moscow. 7 March 1872.

[...] I sincerely rejoice, my friend, that you are finally free to do with yourself as you like.[4] I have complete confidence in you, and I am also confident that you will attain your goal, even if this goal will appear to you in different guises while remaining inwardly the same. I am not surprised that you are now primarily attracted by the sciences: that, in fact, is where one should begin. But then you should go beyond them, for science cannot be the final goal of life. The supreme, true goal of life is moral (or religious) in nature; and science serves only as one of the means to this goal. But it would be better to talk about this when we meet, as well as about the "subordinate" character of women, since the exchange of letters is not a convenient way to treat this disputatious subject. I hope to see you before Holy Week in Kharkov, from where I'll go on to Fyodorovka.[5] I plan to spend about ten days there to breathe the fresh air a little, since in Moscow I find the beginning of spring intolerable. If nothing hinders me, I'll depart as soon as I finish my present studies [...]

Farewell, my dear friend. I hope we can meet soon.

Your Vl. Solovyov.

5.

Moscow. 26 March 1872.

After a *three-month* silence I finally received your letter, dear Katya, the one dated 19 March. [...]

---

4. Ekaterina was approaching the age of seventeen, when she would realize a greater personal freedom under the law.

5. Fyodorovka was the estate of Solovyov's and Ekaterina's grandmother, E. F. Romanova. It is where the friendship of Solovyov and Ekaterina Romanova first blossomed.

You write: "it appears that I am not to blame for anything," etc.; "I was sad when I had to change my opinion," etc. I don't know why you are writing this; I don't know why you don't wish to understand the most simple things. In any case, if you still doubt the constancy of my friendship, I consider it useless to try to convince you of it: you don't really expect me to swear solemnly to it, do you?

If on your part this is only a *manière de parler*, then, please, stop it and be sincere. It would be much better, my dear, if, instead of "pathetic words," you were to write me more of yourself and of our mutual relatives.

What are you doing now? What are your occupations? I sense (with great pleasure) that your interest in the "sciences" has cooled significantly. *Ma foi! und es ist gut!* I am of the opinion that it is even more stupid to study the empty phantoms of external phenomena than it is to *live* by such empty phantoms. But—and this is the main thing—this "science" cannot attain its goal. People look through microscopes, slice up unfortunate animals, boil crud in chemical retorts, and imagine that they are studying *nature*! One should write the following on the foreheads of such asses:

> *Nature does not permit us*
> *To lift her beauty's veil.*
> *And you'll never extract by machine*
> *What your spirit can't divine in her.*[6]

Instead of living nature, they embrace its dead skeletons. We shall discuss this, and much else, when we meet; for I hope to see you (or dream of seeing you) at the end of May, when I fin-

---

6. This is an original poem by Solovyov.

ish my exams and shall be a bird totally free. For the time being I embrace you in my imagination.

Yours always, Vl. Solovyov.

6.

Moscow. 8 July 1872.

You write to me, dear Katya, that my mother has *refused* to be your guardian.[7] I don't know anything about a *refusal*. As far as I know, my mother did no more than write to Grandmother that, in her opinion, *it would be much better for you* to remain in Kharkov. That shouldn't surprise you, since you know that that is the general opinion of all your relations (except me). You know that they consider your desire to pursue your studies a fantasy, which can only bring you harm and ruin your life; and therefore *out of love for you* they are attempting to deflect you from your ruinous intention. Likewise, my mother. When she learned then of your intention to move to Petersburg, she became horrified and said that, if anything, it would be better for you to live in Moscow, but the best thing would be for you to stay in Kharkov. Even now the only reason she is not agreeing to your request is because she thinks that she can thus induce you to stay in Kharkov, since she does not believe you will be absolutely resolute in fulfilling, come what may, your intention. But when it turns out that the matter is settled, that you have parted for good with your aunt, and when you arrive in Moscow, then

---

7. Solovyov's mother did in fact have qualms over his relationship with Ekaterina. Solovyov's parents opposed their marriage because of their close blood-relationship: Solovyov and Ekaterina were first cousins. His parents did not look favorably upon their living in the same household, which the mother's guardianship would have entailed.

you can be certain that my mother will agree to be your guardian, since she has nothing, and can have nothing, against guardianship in and of itself. The only reason my mother does not give her agreement is that she is afraid of facilitating the fulfillment of plans that, in her opinion, are harmful *for you*. But when she becomes convinced that you have decided to fulfill them even without her agreement, she will have no reason to refuse and will not refuse, I can assure you. Therefore, my dear, be tranquil and, in the middle of August, come to Moscow, where, for the moment, you can stay with us in Neskuchnoye[8] (I know for a fact that you can do this even without a guardian; all you need to have is your papers, which are probably already in your possession [...]). If you don't wish to come to Moscow without having an official guardian, you can name someone as a nominal guardian, and then change it to my mother after your arrival. If you don't have anyone in mind, I can mention several people who will agree. Write me your intentions concerning all this.

As for me, there is no way 1 can follow your advice concerning the Caucasus[9]: you know that, in the spring, 1 must take my graduation exam, that is, for all four courses; and therefore time is precious for me. If I were to go anywhere, it would be, of course, not to the Caucasus but to Fyodorovka; but I cannot do even that, despite my desire to. About my health, please don't worry: it will become perfectly well when I become calm, that is, when your business is settled.

Until our meeting, my darling.

Yours entirely. Vl. Solovyov

8. The site of a government dacha used by Solovyov's father and his family.

9. That is, her advice that he travel to the Caucasus.

7.

Moscow. 6 August 1872.

[...] I think you're very angry with her [Solovyov's mother],[10] but let me assure you—it's for naught. She genuinely loves you, and if her view of this matter does not coincide with yours and mine, she is not to blame.

So, come to Moscow. God is my witness that I desire this *only for your sake.* You wish to leave the broad, common path; your kind guardians, who know only this path, are certain that, if you leave it, you will get lost and perish; but I know another path and that you will find it, even though you do not yet know it. Your mere aspiration to leave the false path is a true guarantee that you will find "the way, the truth, and the life."[11]

For the majority of people, these words are empty and meaningless, just as, for the blind, light is an empty, meaningless word. But when you read this I know you will not think I am a mere dreamer.

I have seen a divine spark in you, and I know that it cannot be extinguished. With time, this spark can flame up and become a beneficent light for many in the midst of the impenetrable darkness that prevails in our time.

It might appear that I am making a fly into an elephant, but I stand by this figure: a large fire can start with a small spark.

Farewell, my darling. And may God bless you.

Your Vl. Solovyov

10. Ekaterina's anger is caused by her belief that Solovyov's mother has refused to be her guardian (see letter 6).

11. John 14:6.

11.

Moscow. 31 December 1872.

My dear Katya, today I wish to talk to you about many things, and first about the most important thing. I am much gladdened by your serious attitude toward the most significant (in my opinion, the unique) question of life and knowledge: the question of religion. With reference to this, your present error [...] is that you are confusing faith in general with one of its forms: with blind, childish, unconscious faith, and that you think there's no other faith. Of course, one doesn't need that much intelligence to refute such a faith—I rejected it when I was thirteen years old. Of course, no person who is to any extent a thinking person can believe in the same manner as when he was a child; and if this is a person with a superficial or limited mind, he does not go further than this easy rejection of his childish faith, fully certain that his nanny's fairy tales or elementary phrases of the catechism represent true religion, true Christianity. On the other hand, we know that all the great thinkers—the glory of humanity—have been people of true and profound faith (only windbags like the French Encyclopedists or the contemporary Büchners and Vogts, who have not produced a single original thought, have been atheists). Well-known are the words of Bacon, the founder of positive science: a little mind and a little philosophy lead one away from God, whereas more mind and more philosophy bring one closer to Him again. And although God is one and the same, the faith to which more philosophy leads us is not the same as the faith a little mind leads us away from. It is not hard to see that the faith of a conscious, thinking Christian differs in some manner from the faith of an old peasant woman even though the objects of faith are the same in the two cases and both might be true Christians; and the inner sense of faith in the two is the same. The difference lies in the fact that the old peasant woman does not think at all about the object of her faith, or if she does think about it, it is in concepts that correspond to her intellectual level. Meantime, a conscious Christian, who rationally understands the teaching of Christianity, finds in it a resolution to all the higher questions of knowledge—he finds an abundance and profundity of thought before which all the fabrications of the human mind pale. But it is clear to him that it is not he himself who puts this profound meaning into Christianity; for he is clearly conscious of the complete insignificance and impotence of his mind, of his thought, before the grandeur and power of divine thought. At this time I shall not attempt to explain to you what constitutes this divine content of the Christian idea. For an explanation to be accessible, one must already have completed that inner development which you are only commencing. God grant that you complete it in the way I hope you do! Let me now tell you how a person becomes a conscious Christian.

In childhood, every person receives ready-made beliefs and, of course, believes what he is told. However, for such a belief too what is necessary is, if not an understanding, then some sort of idea of objects of belief. But a child forms for himself ideas of this sort that are more or less absurd; he becomes accustomed to them and considers them inviolably sacred. Many people (and, in past times, almost all people) never abandon such ideas, and live their lives as good people. But the minds of others outgrow their childish beliefs. First with fear, then with complacency, one belief after another is subjected to doubt, is criticized by the semi-childish reason, is found to be absurd, and is rejected. As far as I, personally, am concerned, at this age not only did I experience doubt and reject my former beliefs, but I also hated them with my whole heart—I am ashamed to remember the stupid blasphemies I then spoke and committed. —Ultimately, all beliefs are rejected and the young mind is fully free. Many people go no further than such freedom from all conviction, and are even very proud of it; afterwards they usually become practical men of affairs or crooks. Those who are not capable of such a fate, attempt to establish a new system of convictions to replace the one destroyed, to replace beliefs with rational *knowledge*. And so they turn to positive science, but the latter cannot serve to ground rational convictions, for it does not know anything except external reality, except facts. The true meaning of a fact, a rational explanation of nature and man—science refuses to give. Some turn to abstract philosophy, but the latter remains within the domain of logical thought; reality and life do not exist for abstract philosophy, whereas man's true convictions must be not abstract, but living. They must exist not in the reason alone but in his whole spiritual being. A man must live not only in the ideal world of concepts but also in the real world. Neither science nor philosophy can give such a living conviction. Where can one seek such a conviction? And here a terrifying state of despair comes upon us (even now the memory of it is painful): total inner emptiness, darkness, death in life. All that abstract reason can give, has been experienced and turned out to be worthless; and reason itself has rationally proved its own insolvency. But this darkness is the beginning of light; for when a person is compelled to say: I am nothing, he thereby says: God is all. And here he comes to know God—not as a childish idea and not as an abstract concept; rather, he knows the real, living God, who is "not far from every one of us: for in him we live, and move, and have our being."[12] Then, all the questions that reason posed but could not resolve, find an answer in the profound mysteries of the

12. Acts 17:28.

Christian teaching; and a person now believes in Christ not only because he receives in Him the satisfaction of all the needs of his heart, but also because Christ resolves all the questions of his mind, fulfills all the needs of his knowledge. Faith through hearsay is replaced by faith through reason: cf. the Samaritans in the Gospel: "Now we believe, not because of thy saying: for we have heard him ourselves, and know that this is indeed the Christ, the Saviour of the world."[13]

And so, you see that when a person develops correctly with reference to religion, he progresses through three ages: first, the age of childish or blind faith; then, the development of reason and the rejection of blind faith; and, finally, the age of a conscious faith, based on the development of reason. You now find yourself in the second age. God grant that you reach the third.

But for now let us pass to everyday matters. Your rejection of Prince Dadiani's proposal[14] greatly saddened me: of course, knowing nothing about it, I cannot have a just idea of something that is occurring 700 miles away. But I have a strong feeling that it would have been better for you to have accepted the proposal. If he's a good man, given his riches and his rank, you could have done much good through him and with him that you cannot do alone. In any case, the reasons for the rejection which you give, are very bad. "I do not love him enough," etc. I greatly regret if you believe the rotten fable, invented by rotten scribblers of rotten novels in our rotten age—the fable of some sort of special, supernatural love, which must unite two hearts for mutual bliss, without which it is supposedly impermissible to enter into a law-

13. 2 John 4:42.
14. Ekaterina's rejection of Prince Dadiani, whom she had met during a stay in Odessa, greatly upset her grandmother, who was hoping to assure Ekaterina's security through a good marriage.

ful marriage. On the contrary, a true marriage must be not a means to pleasure or happiness, but a feat of ascesis and self-sacrifice. As for the fact that you supposedly don't like family life— should one always do what one likes or what gives one pleasure?

And so, if the matter is not yet completely settled, then, for God's sake, think well about this.

If you have no other, better reasons, and if my advice means anything, then I decisively and insistently advise you to accept Prince Dadiani's proposal. If you don't like my advice, at least you must admit that it is completely objective.

About rules of propriety and their violation, your reasoning is rather strange. If all such rules are of no importance (as is indubitable), then why violate them? Why struggle against them as if they were important? Why manifest your power only upon trifles? This indicates only pettiness and childishness. Do you really think that a matter as important as freedom of convictions can have anything in common with such nonsense as rules of propriety?

I found even more unpleasant that hostile and almost furious tone in which you spoke about your relatives. If there is little love and meekness in you (but I do not think that is the case), this is very sad and nothing to be proud of [...]

If you do not marry Dadiani (which would be a great pity), I will of course visit Fyodorovka in the summer, if it is allowed. As for the Vienna exhibition, *merci beaucoup*! When we had a polytechnical exhibition in Moscow this past summer, I did not go even once. There's no chance I would go to Vienna. Speaking generally, I am a mortal foe of such exhibitions, at which the accursed civilization of the West admires itself. Moreover, what a strange fantasy: to go to Vienna just the two of us! If you desire to compromise yourself in all manner of ways, then I of course will not offer you any help in this. And you even wrote me about being cautious! But I hope that all this nonsense, all this self-assured childishness will end quickly and harmlessly.

Farewell. Yours always, Vl. Solovyov.

PS. January 1873.

If, in this letter, my darling, there is anything that offends you, you will forgive me, because you know that I love you even more than I should. I request that you answer me as soon as possible. I am greatly interested in the matter of the proposal; moreover, you must know that every line you write is forty thousand times more precious to me than any written or printed paper in the world.

12.

Moscow. 6 June 1873.

[...] my dear friend, in order to tell you anything practical, in order to be of any use to you at all, I must know what your *specific* need is, what *precisely* your state is, *precisely* what questions trouble you. But for now I can give you only one bit of advice: when your thought confronts some question, some doubt, do not abandon this question or doubt until it is defined clearly and precisely, in such a way that you can communicate it to others in a definite form. [...]

Your Vl. Solovyov.

13.

19 July 1873. Okosovo.[15]

I am very glad, dear Katya, that you were surprised by the irritated tone of my last letter. That means that you cannot

15. The site of the estate of the family of Solovyov's friend N.I. Kareev, whom Solovyov was visiting at the time.

guess the reason for my irritation; and therefore this reason is groundless. In any case, these are trifles about which it is not worth speaking.

In one of your letters (dated 7 May of this year), you wrote that, as the goal of your life, you have decided to found a school for the people, since "a few individuals liberated from the terrible ignorance in which the whole of the Russian people finds itself, mean a great deal when there are so few who have been led out of this horrible darkness." I assume that you are quite serious about this matter, and therefore I wish to speak to you about it. I will not touch upon the various practical conditions for the realization of this intention. I will only say a few words about the goal itself of "leading the people out of horrible darkness." *Where* do you see darkness, and where do you see light? You understand, of course, that the ability to read, write, and count is not yet education; the important thing is *what* to read. But what can one propose as reading matter at the present time? Contemporary literature? If you do not know, I will tell you that it is impossible to find a better means of intellectual vulgarization and moral corruption than contemporary literature. The peasants have common sense and will understand at once what the essence of contemporary education is. Its essence, however it may be concealed, consists in the rejection of all spiritual and moral principles and in the affirmation of animal nature alone. The whole wisdom of this age is reduced to a very simple proposition: man is an animal.

Is that the light with which we can illuminate our ignorant people? It is true that the moral state of the common people is very low; that they have fallen nearly to the level of animals. But as long as the people retain the notion of "sin," as long as they know that man *should not* be an animal, they retain the ability to rise to a higher level. But once they are convinced that they have an animal nature and that, by living animalistically, they behave in accordance with their nature—then any possibility of regeneration will disappear. Thank God that this will never happen and that the preachers of animalhood do not have any influence upon the people.

Thus, before thinking about the education or illumination of others, one oneself must possess the light, or at least know where it is to be found. But do you know where it is to be found? In the next letter after the one cited, you ask yourself: "Will I remain in this horrible darkness?"

Thus, you see that you and I are still very far from leading the Russian people out of darkness. We do not even know where the darkness is and where the light is [...].

I don't know why *Crime and Punishment* made you so indignant. Read it to the end; also, it would be beneficial to read all of Dostoevsky.[16] He is one of the few writers of our day and age who has preserved in himself the image and likeness of God.

Farewell. Your Vl. Solovyov

14.

Moscow. 6 July 1873.

[...] I will let my answer be direct: I love you to the extent I am capable of loving. But I belong not to myself but to the work that I will serve. This work does not have anything in common with personal feelings, with the interests and goals of personal life. I cannot give all of myself to you, but to offer less I consider unworthy.

That is all that I can tell you. I wish to know your opinion.

16. On Solovyov's friendship with Dostoevsky see: Marina Kostalevsky, *Dostoevsky and Soloviev: the Art of Integral Vision* (New Haven, 1997).

I will await your letter.

Your Vl. Solovyov.

15.

Moscow. 11 July 1873.

It is sad, my dear Katya, that, even despite our mutual love, we cannot understand each other completely. This, however, is more my fault than yours: whatever the case may be, I will try to speak more clearly. I think that you cannot doubt my love: until now I have not even been able to hide it all that well. But now you give me the opportunity to speak openly: I love you as much as I am capable of loving a human being, and perhaps more strongly than I should. For the majority of people that would be the end of the matter; love and that which must follow it—family happiness—constitutes the main interest of their lives. But I have another task altogether, which with each passing day becomes clearer, more definite, and more rigorous for me. I intend to dedicate my life to fulfilling this task to the extent I am capable of doing so. Personal and family relationships will therefore always occupy a *secondary* place in my existence. That is the only thing I meant when I wrote that I could not give all of myself to you. But that, as I conclude from your last letter, could not change your feelings for me. On my part, although the task about which I am speaking is of a type that cannot be shared with anyone, nevertheless, the sympathy of a loving woman can of course sustain and reinforce one's strength in those difficult labors and life-struggles with which the fulfillment of any serious task is necessarily connected. Such assistance is irreplaceable; and of course I can accept it only from you. But you know, my dear, that our relationship depends not upon us and not upon our love. You know what manner of obstacles prevent our union (although it is somewhat difficult for me to write about this so directly, I must add that I mean only that union which is consecrated by the law and the Church; there can be no question of any other kind of relationship between us). It is very difficult, but possible, to remove these obstacles. In any case, one must do whatever one can to remove them. For now I propose the following: let us wait three years, in the course of which you will undertake your inner education. Meanwhile, I will work upon the laying of a preliminary foundation for the future realization of my main task, while attempting to achieve a certain social position, which I could offer you. If you agree to this, we can discuss it when we meet.

I would like to say much else to you, but words are mute and banal.

Farewell, my darling. Yours always,

Vl. Solovyov.

16.

Moscow. 25 July 1873.

Console me, my darling, my life, Katya: I must yet wait four months for our next meeting.

I had made all preparations to go to Petersburg, but I was asked: Why are you going there *now?* To take care of such and such business, was my response. But in the *summer* there is no business to take care of in Petersburg; the people one needs are not present then: they've all left for the summer. I have to work in the Public Library, I responded. It's a lot better to work there in the winter, I was told, since there's nobody in the Library either. What could I do? Either I would have to admit that I was going to Petersburg solely to see you, that, besides my Katya, I did not need anyone or anything there—but to tell this truth would be an irreparable stupidity. Or I would have to agree with the well-founded arguments mentioned above, and to accept Papa's invitation to travel together with him to Petersburg on December 1st, Sunday, at exactly 8:30 p.m. I agreed and acted prudently, I then thought. But only now, when the matter is settled, do I feel how unbearably painful this prudence is— never have I experienced such excruciating anguish. I know that you too are not in very high spirits, all alone in that lousy empty city. I would have come long ago despite everything if I could have done so without compromising *you*. Yes, it appears that there are not many rosebuds for us to gather on our path. But that's actually good: it's a little embarrassing to be happy; and even more so in our sad age. A painful consolation! It is true that there is an inner world of thought, inaccessible to any of life's accidents or to any of the soul's adversities—a world of thought which is not abstract but alive, and which needs to be actualized. I not only hope but also am certain (as I am of my own existence) that, sooner or later, other people too, indeed all people, will become conscious of the truth that I am conscious of; and that then, with its inner power, this truth will transform this whole world of falsehood, will extirpate forever all the injustice and evil of personal and social life, will extirpate the rude ignorance of the people's masses, the abomination of the moral desolation of the educated classes, the rule of fist between states—that abyss of darkness, filth, and blood in which mankind is thrashing even until now. All this will vanish like a nocturnal phantom before the light of Christ's eternal truth rising in our consciousness, a truth that, till now, has not been understood or accepted by mankind; and the kingdom of God will come in all its glory, the kingdom of inner spiritual relationships, of pure love and joy—a new heaven and a new earth, in which justice lives. But it is impossible for insignificant man to live constantly in this world that exists only in thought but has not yet been actualized for us. And once again the heart feels heavy anguish and dull suffering. And even more unbearable become the petty obstacles and collisions, all these slaps in the face from everyday life.

My joy, my darling, in these moments of the soul's fatigue, weakness, and despair, only your love can sustain and encourage me. Remind me of your love more frequently, I implore you. I do not yet fully believe in it; forgive me.

Yours forever, Vl. Solovyov.

18.

Moscow. 2 August 1873.

I had just sent out my complaint concerning your silence, my dear friend Katya, when I received your letter, which filled me with boundless joy. (But don't think that I gave outward expression to my joy: when I receive your letters, I am indifference personified. In general, I become much more restrained then; I become slyness itself, I assure you: I wish to be as wise as a serpent and as harmless as a dove.)[17] As far as our relationship is concerned, I have given you and am continuing to give you—whether you want it or not—my word, about which you speak. Am I capable of deceiving you? You will find that out empirically in the future—there is no need to talk about it.

Let me attempt to give a better answer to your question (insofar as that is possible in a single letter) about my goal and my occupations. Since the time I reached the age of understanding, I have been aware that the existing order of things (primarily the social and civil order, the relationships among people

17. Cf. Matt. 10:16.

that determine the whole of human life) is far from being as it *should* be, that it is based not on reason and law but, for the most part, on meaningless accident, blind force, egotism, and compulsory subordination. Although practical people see the inadequacy of such an order (it is impossible not to see it), they find it possible and convenient to adapt to it, to find a cozy place for themselves in it and to live as best they can. Others are incapable of reconciling themselves with the world's evil; but they consider it necessary and eternal, and must content themselves with impotently despising the existing reality or cursing it à la Lord Byron. Such people are very noble, but their nobility does not change anything. I belong to neither group. The conscious conviction that the present state of mankind is *not as it should be* signifies for me that it *must be changed*, transformed. I do not recognize the existing evil to be eternal; I do not believe in the devil. Since I am conscious of the necessity of transformation, I oblige myself to dedicate my entire life and all my powers to making sure that this transformation is accomplished. But the most important thing is: *where are the means* to it? To be sure, there are people for whom this problem seems very simple and the task an easy one. They *do* see (though very superficially and narrowly) that the existing order of things is inadequate, but they believe they can change things by fighting fire with fire, i.e., by destroying compulsion by compulsion, injustice by injustice, by wiping away blood with blood. They wish to regenerate mankind by murders and arsons. They may be very good people but they are very poor musicians. God will forgive them, for they know not what they do. I understand the matter differently. I know that all transformations must come *from within*, from the human mind and heart. People are governed by their *convictions*; and therefore it is necessary to act upon their convictions, to convince people of the truth. Truth itself, i.e.,

Christianity (of course, not that pseudo-Christianity which we all know from various catechisms), is clear in my consciousness, but the question is how to incorporate it in the universal consciousness, for which, at the present time, it is a sort of *monstrum*—something utterly alien and incomprehensible. One asks first of all: What is the source of this alienation of the contemporary mind from Christianity? To blame human error or ignorance for everything would be very easy, and just as frivolous. The cause is deeper-lying. The fact of the matter is that, although Christianity is, in itself, absolutely true, it has hitherto received a very one-sided and insufficient expression as a result of historical conditions. With the exception of certain elite minds, for the majority Christianity has been an affair of mere semiconscious faith and indeterminate feeling, but has said nothing to *reason*, has not been embraced by reason. As a result, Christianity has been imprisoned in an irrational form inappropriate to it, and a lot of meaningless rubbish has been heaped upon it. And when it grew up and escaped into freedom from the medieval monasteries, human reason was right to rise up against *such* Christianity and to reject it. But now, after the pseudo-Christianity has been destroyed, the time has come to restore the true one. The task is to put the eternal content of Christianity into a new form appropriate to it, i.e., an unconditionally rational form. To accomplish this it is necessary to use everything that has been developed by the human mind in recent centuries: it is necessary to study all of philosophy. I am doing this and will continue to do it. It is now as clear to me as twice two equals four that the entire grand evolution of Western philosophy and science—which on the surface appears to be indifferent to and often hostile to Christianity—has actually worked out a new, worthy form for Christianity. And when Christianity is truly expressed in this new form, when it is manifested in its true aspect, then we shall see the spontaneous dis-appearance of that which has hitherto prevented it from being incorporated in the universal consciousness: its apparent con-tradiction with reason. When Christianity is manifested as light and reason, it will necessarily become a universal conviction, or at least the conviction of all those who have something in their head or heart. When Christianity becomes an actual conviction, i.e., one by which people *live*, then *all will clearly change*. Imag-ine what would happen if a certain (even a very small) portion of mankind were actually to fulfill the teaching of absolute love and self-sacrifice in all seriousness, with a strong conscious con-viction. Would injustice and evil then persist for long in the world?—But we are still far from such a practical realization of Christianity in the world. We must yet diligently work on the theoretical aspect, on the theological doctrine. That constitutes my present work. You probably know that this year I will study theology at a religious academy, where I plan to live. Some peo-ple are imagining that I wish to become a monk and am even aiming at the archbishopric. Let them: I won't try to undeceive them. But you can see that that does not at all fit into my plans. Monasticism did at one time have a high calling, but now the time has come not to flee the world but to go into the world in order to transform it.

You understand, my friend, that with such convictions and intentions I must seem totally crazy, and, like it or not, I must be restrained. But that does not embarrass me: "the foolishness of God is wiser than men."[18]

Farewell, my darling. With hopes for a meeting, yours always,

Vl. Solovyov.

18. 1 Cor. 1:25.

19.[19]

[...] In 2 weeks I will move to Sergiev Posad,[20] where I will live utterly alone. I have many plans and hopes for the winter. The majority of them will, of course, not be realized. But I feel no lack of boldness and self-confidence. For the time being I will astound good people with my holy foolishness. Even now I inspire doubt and confusion: some consider me a nihilist; others—a religious fanatic; still others—a madman. I hope to inspire even more doubt and confusion later on. After 2 months I will begin ploughing in Moscow (and a year later in Petersburg) —at first not a very large field, but one with very loose soil, on which, it is true, nothing but burdock and nettles have grown so far, but on which good grain can grow if the sowing is done properly. I write allegorically because one should not write directly about what does not yet exist and perhaps will not exist. If I am right, you will know more in 2 months. [...] Farewell, my dear, until our meeting in 114 days.

Your Vl. Solovyov.

20.

Moscow, 10 August 1873.

I wrote you that I'm becoming sly. Since I'm not used to it, I have not been very successful. Sometimes I'm caught at it in the most humorous fashion. And sometimes I don't want to pretend: it's as if I'm trying to cover up something bad.

What you wrote me, my dear Katya, about the proposal[21]

19. Undated. Sent from Moscow.
20. The site of the Moscow Theological Academy at the Trinity-St. Sergius Lavra, where Solovyov was to attend lectures.
21. Ekaterina had received a proposal from Vasily Passek, a relative of hers by marriage.

you received I found very unpleasant—partly because of my senseless ugly jealousy, which afflicts me whenever anyone else even pronounces your name, let alone makes you a proposal. But mainly I found it unpleasant because it is very, very difficult to stride over others and, dreaming of the salvation of mankind, to become—through a cruel irony of life—the involuntary cause of someone else's unhappiness. [...] Everything that you write about my goals is completely right. But you wrongly imagine that I dream of some instantaneous regeneration of mankind. I will not, in any case, see the living fruit of my future labors. For myself personally I foresee nothing good. At best, I will be considered crazy. But this is not something I think about much. Success will come sooner or later—that's sufficient for me.

We must fulfill our duty—that is all we can do. To determine the times and seasons is not our task. Sometimes the very distant seems near to the mind; this is good, because it is comforting...

Farewell, my soul.

Your Vl. Solovyov.

P.S. How strangely you put it: that you are afraid to annoy me with your chatter.

22.

26 August 1873.

[...] I don't know why you find it so unpleasant that I live like a hermit, that is, that I avoid meaningless amusements and don't give myself to debauchery. It must be that someone has told you lies about me. With regard to your suspicions, I can only remark that our separation has been sufficiently long for any "momentary infatuation" to have passed; I have had momentary infatuations, and I know the difference.

As for my opinion about the ability of women to understand the higher truth, I affirm that there is no doubt that they indeed have this ability; otherwise they would not be human beings. But the fact of the matter is that, because of their passive nature, women *cannot find this truth themselves*, but must receive it from men. It is a fact that no religious or philosophical doctrine has been founded by a woman, but, *once they have been founded*, doctrines have been assimilated and propagated primarily by women. I assume that women will also play an important role in the coming revolution in the consciousness of humankind. But this revolution will begin where nobody is expecting it. You've written to me about the sect of Stundists[22] (I am delighted that your attention was drawn to this); this sect is not unique—a similar movement can be seen in other places too: for example, there is a sect of spiritual Christians called the "sighers" in the province of Kaluga, etc. The peasant will soon display his true power to the great confusion of those who see in him nothing but drunkenness and crude superstition (you too, my friend, were once guilty of such an opinion). Glorious and difficult times are approaching, and happy are those who can await them with hope, not with fear. Farewell, my dear friend. Would it be possible for us to see each other before December? What do you think? Mama said that she would be very glad if you could come visit us; at that time I will be living, you understand, at the Trinity-St. Sergius Lavra. By the way, in answer to your question: 1 will probably live there only this year, i.e., until June, and then whatever God grants.

Your Vl. Solovyov.

---

22. Russian Protestants who emphasized evangelical piety.

24.

Sergiev Posad, 15 September 1873.

My dearest Katya!

Your letter which I've just received has provoked such unusual joy in me that I started talking loudly with the German philosophers and Greek theologians who, in touching harmony, populate my dwelling. They have never before seen me in such indecorous ecstasy; and one fat father of the Church even fell from the table from indignation.

I was, after all, completely certain that everything between us was over, and could not imagine how and for what reason that had happened. [;]

28.[23]

My darling Katya, my joy, I wish to dedicate this night to a conversation with you; in the early morning I need to go to the train station, and in order not to oversleep I prefer not to go to bed at all.

I now find myself in a fairly curious state. In the Academy my arrival produced the same impression as the arrival of the supposed Inspector General in that famous town "from which you can ride for three years without getting to any state."[24] The professors here imagine that I have arrived with the sole purpose of disturbing their tranquility with my criticism. All are extremely amiable with me, like the mayor with Khlestakov.[25] Grateful for this, I leave them in peace as much as I can (although the lectures that I have attended so far have been

23. Undated. Sent from Sergiev Posad.
24. A reference to Gogol's comedy *The Inspector General*.
25. The protagonist of Gogol's *The Inspector General*.

quite good). But they themselves put a very low value on themselves and their work, and cannot believe that an outsider, a member of the gentry and a doctoral candidate of the University, could have gotten it into his head to study the theological sciences. I am, in fact, the first example of this they have seen; and therefore they suppose that I have some special practical purpose in mind. The Academy in any case is not as absolutely vacuous as the University. With all their crudeness, the students seem to be pretty intelligent; they are also amiably merry and are masters at having a drink—good hearty souls, the truth be told. But I won't have time to become pals with them.

Although you didn't ask me about my studies, I feel obliged to give an account of them. First of all, I'm writing an article titled "The History of the Religious Consciousness in the Ancient World"[26] (the first part is already going to appear in a journal). In this work my purpose is to explain the ancient religions; without such an explanation one cannot fully understand world history in general and Christianity in particular. Secondly, I'm continuing to study the Germans and am writing an article (also for a journal) about the contemporary crisis of Western philosophy.[27] This article will later become part of my master's dissertation, a synopsis of which I have already written. Thirdly, I'm reading the Greek and Latin theologians of the ancient Church. Without their study too, a full understanding of Christianity is impossible.

These are only initial, preliminary studies; the true work lies ahead. Without this work, without this great task, I have no

---

26. This evolved into Solovyov's first published work: "The Mythological Process in Ancient Paganism" (1873).

27. This grew into Solovyov's first published monograph: *The Crisis of Western Philosophy: Against the Positivists* (1874).

reason to live. Without it, I would not dare to love you. I would have no right to you were I not fully certain that I could give you what others cannot give you. You have seen and can always see at your feet a great many men who have all the external advantages over me. For the time being, I am nothing...[28]

In the lines crossed out, I wrote what I should not have written. It's better not to continue.

Farewell. Your Vl. Solovyov.

28. Nine lines were crossed out in the original.

Three Meetings

Editor's Note

ALTHOUGH Soloyvov's three encounters with Sophia took place in the 1860s and 1870s, he waited until 26–29 September 1898 to compose his celebrated long sophianic poem, "Three Meetings." The present translation is a slightly revised version of the translation presented in *The Religious Poetry of Vladimir Solovyov*, Semantron Press, 2008.

Thematically, "Three Meetings" has much in common with Solovyov's sophianic story, "At The Dawn of Mist-Shrouded Youth."

Three Meetings[1]

(Moscow-London-Egypt, 1862-75-76)

Triumphing beforehand over death
And through love having overcome the chain
Of aeons, eternal beloved, I will not name you,
But my tremulous song will reach your ears.

Not believing the deceitful world,
Beneath the rough crust of matter
I have touched the incorruptible royal purple
And recognized the radiance of divinity...

Have you not thrice appeared to my real sight?
You have not been a figment of the mind,
O no! As portent, help, or as reward,
Your image has come to answer my soul's call.

1.

The first time—but how long ago that was!
Thirty-six years have passed since my soul,
Then childish, unexpectedly felt love's longing
Together with the anxiety of dark dreams.

---

1. I have consulted the translation of "Three Meetings" included in Paul M. Allen's *Vladimir Soloviev: Russian Mystic*, Blauvelt, New York, 1978, pp. 345–357. I have also consulted Judith Deutsch Kornblatt's translation, "Three Encounters," as well as her notes (MS, 1997).

I was nine years old, and she[2]... she was nine too.
"It was a day in May in Moscow," as Fet[3] wrote.
I then confessed my love. Silence. O God!
I have a rival. He will answer to me!
A duel! A duel! At the Ascension Feast service
A stream of passionate torments coursed through my soul.
Let us lay aside... all earthly cares: drawn out,
These words of the hymn faded gradually and stopped.

The sanctuary was open... But where were priest and deacon?
Where was the crowd of praying people? Suddenly,
The stream of passions dried up without a trace.
Azure was all around; azure was in my soul.

Suffused with a golden azure, and your hand
Holding a flower that came from other lands,
You stood there smiling a smile of radiance.
You nodded to me, and vanished in the mist.

With that the childish love grew far removed
From me, my soul grew blind to earthly things...
My German nurse kept on repeating sadly:
"Volodinka, ach, how he has stupid become!"[4]

2. The "she" here is just a little girl who has nothing in common with the "eternal beloved" to whom the introduction is addressed. The episode of the "duel" has an autobiographic character.

3. This is a paraphrase of Afanasy Fet's (1820–1892) verse "It was a marvelous day in May in Moscow." Fet, one of the best Russian poets of the second half of the nineteenth century, was a close friend of Solovyov's.

4. The German nurse speaks ungrammatical Russian here, using a feminine ending as the predicate to "he." The incorrectness of her speech is suggested by word order that is inappropriate in English. Volodinka is a diminutive of Vladimir.

2.

Years passed by. A docent and a master,
I rushed abroad for the first time... Berlin,
Then Hanover, Cologne all glimmered past,
In rapid motion hiding from my sight.

Not the world's center, Paris, not Spain,
Nor the Orient's bright multicolored splash—

Rather, the British Museum[5] was my dream.
Nor did this place at all deceive my hopes.

Will I ever forget you, blissful half-year?
Fleeting beauty's phantoms meant nothing to my soul,
Nor did people's lives here, passions, nature.
All my soul was possessed by you alone, beloved.

Despite people's scurrying back and forth in droves
Under the din of fire-breathing machines,
Despite massive soulless edifices all around,
I am immersed in sacred quiet. I am here alone.

Cum grano salis, to be sure: I was
Alone, but surely not a misanthrope.
For people still did find their way to me.
And whom among these people should I mention?

---

5. Solovyov studied mystical literature at the library of the British
Museum from the end of June to the middle of October 1875.

A pity. I do not know how to put
Their names or foreign talk into my meter.
Among them were two or three British scholars
And two or three docents[6] from Moscow. Still,

I was often alone in the reading room,
And, credit this or not, God is my witness
That mysterious powers led me to choose for reading
Everything possible concerning her.

Whenever some sinful whim suggested to me
To open up a book "from another opera,"

Such trouble would ensue from this
That, quite confused, I'd leave for home.

But once—it was in autumn—I said to her:
"O blossoming of divinity! I feel
Your presence here. But why have you not revealed
Yourself to my eyes since I was a child?"

Hardly had I thought these words
When all around was filled with golden azure
And before me she was shining again—
But only her face, it was her face alone.

That instant was one of happiness much prolonged.
My soul again became blind to things of earth.

6. While in England Solovyov made the acquaintance of W. Ralston
(1829–1889), a writer and employee of the British Museum; and the zoolo-
gist Wallace (1822–1913). He also made the acquaintance of two Russian
docents who were law scholars: I. I. Yanzhul (1846–1914) and M. M. Kova-
levsky (1851–1916).

And if I spoke, any "sober" ear
Would consider my speech incoherent and stupid.

3.

I said: "Your face has been revealed to me.
But I would still wish to see all of you.
You were not stingy with the child, and so
Why is it that you should refuse the youth?"

"Go then to Egypt!" sounded a voice inside me.
To Paris! And then steampower bore me southward.
Feeling did not have to fight with reason:
Reason remained quite silent—like an idiot.

To Lyons, Turin, Piacenza, and Ancona,
To Fermo, Bari, then to Brindisi.
Behold: across the shimmering deep-blue
I found myself being sped by a British steamer.

Credit and lodging were offered to me in Cairo
By Hotel Abbat—alas, no longer there!
A cozy, modest hotel, best in the world...
Russians were staying there, even some from Moscow.

A retired general entertained us there
With memories of his old Caucasus days.
It does no harm to name him—he's long dead.
And I have only good things to say about him.

He was the well-known Rostislav Faddeev,[7]
Retired soldier, good man with a pen.
Excellent at remembering names of coquettes.
Knowledgeable, too, about the local cathedrals.

Twice daily we sat together at the table d'hôte.
He was loquacious, he spoke merrily,
Was ever ready with some dubious anecdote,
And, in his limited way, philosophized.

I waited, meanwhile, for the promised meeting,
And suddenly, one night when all was still,
I heard, just like the wind's cool breath, these words:
"I am there in the desert. Go to meet me."

I had to walk. (For one is not transported
From London to the Sahara for nothing.
A marble might have rolled round my empty pocket—
For days on end I had been living on credit.)

God alone knew whither, without provisions
And without money, one fine day, I went,
Like Uncle Vlas, composed without revisions
By Nekrasov. (There, I've somehow found a rhyme.)[8]

7. Rostislav Faddeev (1824–1883) was a general of the Russian army
(retired 1868) and a military writer.
8. The device of finding a rhyme is one that is hallowed by Pushkin's
example. The use of this device here is the more forgivable in that the author,
being not so much young as inexperienced, is making his first try at a narrative poem.—Solovyov's note. [Nikolai Nekrasov (1821–1878), one of the
most celebrated writers of his time, was known mainly for civic and political
verse.]

Surely, you must have been laughing at me when I,
Attired in tall top-hat and warm overcoat in the desert,
Was taken, by sturdy bedouins, for a demon,
Provoking a shiver of fear in them and thus

Was nearly killed. When, in the Arab manner, noisily,
Sheiks of two tribes held a council to decide
My fate, then later tied my hands together
Like a slave's and without mincing words

Led me some distance off, and generously
Untied my hands—and then departed. Now
I'm laughing with you, my beloved: gods and men alike
Can laugh at troubles once they've passed.

By that time the mute night had descended
Directly to the earth. Around me I heard
Only the silence, and saw the darkness
Between the little starry flames.

Lying upon the ground, I looked and listened...
I heard the sinister wailing of a jackal,
Who was dreaming, most likely, of devouring me,
And I'd not brought even a stick to ward him off.

Yet worse than the jackal was the piercing cold...
It now was zero perhaps, and yet the day had been hot.
The stars shined mercilessly clear.
Their shining and the cold warred with my sleep.

Long I lay there in a frightened slumber, till
At last, I heard a gentle whisper: "Sleep, my poor friend."

SOPHIA, GOD & A SHORT TALE ABOUT THE ANTICHRIST

Then I fell into a deep sleep; and when I waked
The fragrance of roses wafted from earth and heaven.

And in the purple of the heavenly glow
You gazed with eyes full of an azure fire.[9]
And your gaze was like the first shining
Of universal and creative day.

What is, what was, and what will be were here
Embraced within that one fixed gaze... The seas
And rivers all turned blue beneath me, as did
The distant forest and the snow-capped mountain heights.

I saw it all, and all of it was one,
One image there of beauty feminine...
The immeasurable was confined within that image.
Before me, in me, you alone were there.

O radiant one! I'm not deceived by you.
I saw all of you there in the desert...
And in my soul those roses shall not fade
Wherever it is the billows of life may rush me.

A single instant! Then the vision was hidden
And into heaven's dome the solar sphere began its rise.
The desert was silent, but my soul was praying
And church bells kept on ringing in my soul.

9. A paraphrase of a line from Lermontov's poem "How often when surrounded by a motley crowd."

My spirit was strong! But for two days I'd fasted
And visions of higher things began to fade.
Alas! However sensitive one's soul,
Starvation never can be a friend, they say.

Toward the Nile I followed the sun's westward path,
And in the evening I returned to Cairo.
Though my soul preserved the traces of your rosy smile,
Many holes had worn their way into my boots.

Viewed from the outside it was all quite stupid.
(I gave the facts but I concealed the vision.)
After he ate his soup quite wordlessly,
The general, gaze fixed at me, grandly began:

"While intelligence gives one the right to be stupid,
It's surely better not to abuse the privilege:
All told, people's obtuseness isn't quite adept
At drawing distinctions between types of madness.

And therefore, if it would offend you
If anyone considered you demented
Or merely a fool, then make no further mention
Of this inglorious adventure to anyone."

His witty utterances flowed on, but before me
The azure mist kept sending out its radiance,
And, defeated by the mysterious beauty,
The ocean of humdrum life receded far away.

Still slave of this vain world, this then was how
Beneath the rough crust of matter, I came to see
The incorruptible royal purple
And felt the radiance of divinity.

Overcoming death by premonition,
Through dreams having triumphed over the chain
Of aeons, eternal beloved, I will not name you,
But pardon, for your part, my feeble song!

(26–29 September 1898)

AUTHOR'S NOTE: The autumn evening and the dense woods inspired me to reproduce in comic verse the most significant thing that had ever happened in my life. For two days the memories and accords rose up irrepressibly in my consciousness. And on the third day this short autobiography, which has pleased some poets and some ladies, was ready.

The Concept of God

In Defense of Spinoza's Philosophy

Editor's Note

"THE CONCEPT OF GOD" was written in 1897 in response to Professor Aleksandr Ivanovich Vvedensky's article, "The Atheism of Spinoza's Philosophy" in *Voprosy filosofii i psikhologii*, book 37, 1897, and perhaps constitutes Solovyov's last thoughts on the theology of God. A scholar of Russian philosophy has written that "Solovyov's defense of Spinoza's religious doctrine... [is]... a defense of the integrity of his own religious philosophy, in anticipation of similar accusations of pantheism that would inevitably be leveled against him."[1]

This translation first appeared in *The Concept of God: Essays on Spinoza* by Aleksandr Vvedensky and Vladimir Solovyov, The Variable Press, 1999. The present translation is a slightly revised version of the earlier one.

BORIS JAKIM

1. Robert Bird, Introduction, *The Concept of God: Essays on Spinoza* by Aleksandr Vvedensky and Vladimir Solovyov, The Variable Press, 1999.

Authors' Note

PROFESSOR Aleksandr Ivanovich Vvedensky must be credited with the rare ability to raise and formulate in an acute manner philosophical questions of the greatest vital interest for thinking people. However one might view the solutions he offers to such questions, their clear formulation is already an important contribution to the philosophical literature. The esteemed professor's latest article, "The Atheism of Spinoza's Philosophy" (in *Voprosy filosofii i psikhologii*, book 37, 1897), appears to me to be such an achievement, although I completely disagree with the views expressed in it—both of Spinoza's doctrine in particular and of the concept of God in general. Professor Vvedensky's achievement consists of a clear and distinct formulation of the following question: What exactly is conceived in the concept of God and what are the conditions of thought under which this concept is actually present in our mind and in the absence of which it disappears, leaving only an empty word? I must confess that Professor Vvedensky's article cut me to the quick, first because of Spinoza (who was my first love in the domain of philosophy), and then because of something more important.

The Concept of God

(*In Defense of Spinoza's Philosophy*)

I

ACCORDING TO Spinoza's definition, as Professor Vvedensky reminds us, God is an absolutely infinite entity, that is, a substance consisting of infinitely many attributes, each of which expresses an eternal and infinite essence. In connection with this, Spinoza denies in God purposive activity and free will, and therefore personal being in the generally accepted sense of this word. From this Professor Vvedensky concludes that Spinoza's philosophy is an atheistic philosophy. Although, in his *Ethics*, the philosopher constantly speaks of God, giving this name to His absolute substance, he *does not have the right* to do so, for he does not have the concept of God. Professor Vvedensky states the following:

> [T]here is no doubt that everyone has the right to understand God in his own way, but only up to a certain limit, namely, only so long as we do not contradict those characteristics which pertain to God *in general*, that is, to *every* God. For the conception of God must be subject to the same logical requirements as the conception of anything else: concerning any particular thing we have the right to think only what does not contradict the concept of that thing. That the right to conceive God in one's own way is limited by a similar restriction

is evident from the consideration that, if the converse were true, nothing would prevent us from agreeing to understand by the word "God" anything whatsoever— for example, matter—and denying the existence of every other God. And in the absence of any restriction on the right to conceive God in one's own way, no one could charge us with atheism. This, however, is a manifest absurdity.[2]

That is perfectly true. The right of everyone to understand God in his own way indisputably has its limit, which is set by the essential characteristics of this concept, in the absence of which it loses all its content. But how can one find these characteristics? According to Professor Vvedensky, that common thing that is attributed to God in all existing religions, the common thing in which all these religions converge, is the thing that will express the inalienable essence of the concept. He writes the following:

> Let us then consider the characteristics which would be common to Zeus and Perun, to the Mohammedan God, the Christian God, and the God of the fetish worshippers, etc. They will be the characteristics which make up the concept of God *in general*, that is, those characteristics which no one can contradict without committing a logically inadmissible equivocation, however he may understand God in other respects.

The first general characteristic of any God is that he always surpasses man to a greater or lesser degree. The Christian God

2. Aleksandr Vvedensky, "The Atheism of Spinoza's Philosophy," trans. George Kline in *The Concept of God: Essays on Spinoza* by Aleksandr Vvedensky and Vladimir Solovyov, The Variable Press, 1999, pp. 3–4.

infinitely surpasses man; Zeus surpasses man to a considerable degree, but not infinitely; and the gods of the fetish-worshippers surpass man even less than Zeus. But every God is conceived as surpassing man to a greater or lesser degree. The immortality which is ascribed to gods may be regarded as an element of this superiority.

A second characteristic of God in general is that he is always conceived as a personal being (comprising either one person, as is generally the case, or three persons, as in the case of the Christian God), who acts purposively and consequently possesses free will. Some gods act purposively in conformity to a moral law; such, for example, is the Christian God. Others, like Zeus, act more or less purposively, but according to caprice. However, every god, in whatever religion, is invariably conceived as acting purposively. Even the fetish-worshippers ascribe purposive action to their fetishes.

Such are two of the characteristics which are contained in the concept of any God whatever, regardless of religious differences. To omit either of these characteristics is to destroy the concept of God in general. As a matter of fact, if we omit the characteristic of superiority, the concept of God will be indistinguishable from that of an outstanding human being, or even an animal, if we admit personhood and purposive action in the latter. And if we omit personhood and purposive action, the concept of God will cease to be distinguishable from that of matter or any vast natural force which surpasses man in an obvious way—for example, a hurricane.

To ignore, that is, to eliminate, these characteristics which are essential to the concept of God in general, and at the same time to employ the word "God," is to equivocate. But that is precisely what Spinoza does. Only one of these characteristics—superiority to man—is included in his concept of God, since by his definition God is a being absolutely infinite. But he constantly attempts to eliminate the second characteristic—that of personhood acting purposively and possessing free will. He thus destroys the concept of God even as he uses it.[3]

However, this argument, whose clarity cannot be denied, provokes some very substantial objections. We do not think that all gods act purposively and we believe that Professor Vvedensky puts too heavy an emphasis on this feature, which he considers to be a distinguishing characteristic of divinity. Having set as his goal the abstraction of a certain concept of God from all existing religions, he ignores religions that do not conform to this goal, while modifying the character of religions he finds insufficiently suitable for his needs.

Southern Buddhism, which has preserved the original doctrine of Sakyamuni[4] and his apostles and has remained the dominant religion of Ceylon, Nepal, and the greater part of IndoChina, has no place for a personal entity as an object of divine worship. To recognize such an entity as the cause of the world is considered by this doctrine to be a great error and dishonesty. "Isvarika," that is, a follower of Isvara, of a personal God in general, is a swear-word for orthodox Buddhists. Orthodox Buddhists do not worship any Isvara, and, admitting the existence of a multitude of fantastical beings whose activity is more or less purposive, they do not place any value on these beings, but put their *trust* only in Buddha—a man, who has saved people by his teaching and who is *detached from all personhood, will, and activity in the absolute peace and indifference of nirvana.*[5]

3. Ibid, pp. 4–5.
4. One of the names of Buddha.—TR.
5. If Professor Vvedensky does not trust on this point the host of European and Russian scholars who have investigated Buddhism, let him turn to

To be sure, Professor Vvedensky can, following the example of many scholars, call this religion atheism (although that
would be untrue); he could prefer northern Buddhism with its
enormous pantheon to southern Buddhism. But that does not
change the situation. Professor Vvedensky asserts that, from *all*
religions without exception, he has abstracted two essential
characteristics which are equally and jointly necessary for the
concept of God: superiority to man and personal, purposive
will. These characteristics should be present in *every* religion
without exception. But we have found a religion, with world-
historical significance, which decisively contradicts Professor
Vvedensky's assertion. The two characteristics that for Professor Vvedensky must be *jointly* present in all religions are
sharply and consistently *separated* from each other in the concepts of orthodox Buddhists. These strange people—who without any difficulty inherited from the earlier religion a multitude
of human-like and animal-like gods who act in a more or less
purposive, though monstrous, manner—once and for all took
away from these gods the characteristic of essential superiority
to man and all higher rights with respect to him. And these
strange people recognized a new object of the religious relation,
a certain absolutely superior entity, being, or state,[6] but one that
is necessarily characterized by a total absence of will, goal,

the catechism of southern Buddhism, which is officially approved by the
hierarch of the Ceylon Buddhists, and he will see that, in this religion, there
is no place for a personal God. There appears to be a Russian-language version of this catechism, which was composed by an American who had
openly converted from Christianity to Buddhism.—Solovyov's note.

6. I am deliberately expressing myself vaguely here, in order to convey
more accurately the Buddhist idea. The words I use refer both to nirvana
and to the perfect Buddha, who has attained Nirvana. This accords with the
Buddhist demand that the subject not be differentiated from the object.—
Solovyov's note.

activity, and personhood. To regard such a doctrine as atheism would be an obvious injustice. The divinity of nirvana is not an empty word, although it is completely clear that this concept contradicts the concept of divinity that Professor Vvedensky considers to be absolutely obligatory.

I have no doubt that Buddhism in general, and southern Buddhism in particular, is a one-sided and insufficient religion; so as not to argue over words, I am prepared to call it outright a false religion. But when conclusions are drawn from the agreement about something of *all* existing religions, it is clear that we must take this religion into account too, no matter how it might repel us. It would be a childish equivocation to assert that a doctrine that for 2000 years has traditionally subordinated to itself the consciousness and life of thirty or forty million people is not a religion.

II

Another important religion that contradicts Professor Vvedensky's conclusion is Brahmanism, a doctrine for which the Vedas (in the broad sense, including the Upanishads) are the supreme sacred authority. Brahmanism is a very complex religion, or a combination of religions united by a common scripture and a caste of Brahmins that preserves this scripture. A great diversity of beliefs and cults, of various origins and from various epochs, characterized by conceptions that can be monstrously wild or subtly philosophical, coexist on this common foundation. One has no need to untangle this diversity when there is a common religious foundation in the sacred Upanishads, just as, in defining the Islamic concept of God, one has no need to untangle the various mythological conceptions involving Ali, the Caliph Hakem, and other "imams." It is sufficient to familiarize oneself with the Koran and the generally accepted traditions closest to Mohammed.

The sacred teaching of the Upanishads, condescendingly treating the various popular gods and the ritual worship of these gods, decisively rises above this "religion of works" and addresses the one true being of all, the infinite world soul, in which *all is one and the same*, in which all separateness and particularity, all particular and individual differences, are annulled. This all-soul or all-spirit (*atma*) is not the same sort of purely negative absoluteness as the Buddhist nirvana. The sacred texts of the Brahmins attribute to the absolute being all possible positive qualities, physical and psychic, in infinite potency. There is only one thing they do not attribute to it: activity on the basis of free will and directed toward specific goals. The authors of the Upanishads probably did not consider this a positive quality. Because they held such a view Professor Vvedensky has to consider them atheists. Let them keep repeating until they are exhausted: "true divinity is the all and the all is true divinity," thus showing themselves to be out-and-out *pantheists* in the most exact and strict sense of the word. That will not help them, just as it will not help them that they attribute absolute thought and omniscience to divinity. After all, Spinoza too recognized, together with extension, infinite *thought* as a necessary attribute of the absolute substance, which possesses above that, in his opinion, an infinite number of other infinite attributes or essential properties. However, all this qualitative and quantitative abundance does not prevent Professor Vvedensky from accusing Spinoza's philosophy of atheism solely because Spinoza denied in the divine substance activity that is purposive and based on free will. But on this point there is no difference between Spinozism and the religious doctrine of the sacred Upanishads. Therefore, one should either recognize both doctrines to be *pantheistic* (as has always been done, and correctly so) or accuse the religion of the Brahmins of *atheism* together with Spinoza's philosophy. But in this case it may be necessary to take the very concept of pantheism out of circulation. In passing, Professor Vvedensky indicates that the essence of this concept lies in the immanence of divinity in things, or the world. But is such an immanence compatible with the second characteristic of the concept of God that he asserts? In what way can a personal being in Professor Vvedensky's sense, that is, as possessing free will and acting purposively and therefore outside itself, be immanent at the same time, that is, inwardly present in something that is not it itself but only an object of its action? In order not to lapse into an equivocation, Professor Vvedensky must recognize as impersonal a divinity that is immanent in things and therefore admit that pantheism, which asserts such an impersonal divinity, rejects the very concept of God and is the same thing as atheism. But in this case it is necessary to exclude from circulation the very term "pantheism," for it is a source of serious misunderstandings. But established and generally accepted philosophical categories cannot be destroyed as easily as old styles of paper money.

III

Not only does Professor Vvedensky fail to mention Buddhism and Brahmanism, his characterization of Christianity is insufficiently accurate. After stating that God is conceived as a *personal being*, Professor Vvedensky adds in brackets "*comprising* either one person, as is generally the case, or *three persons*, as in the case of the Christian God"[7] (the italics are mine). Since the

---

7. Vvedensky, "The Atheism of Spinoza's Philosophy," p. 4.

Christian God is incorporeal, the word "person"[8] should be understood here not as a physical countenance but only as a metaphysical and moral *person*. The expression "a personal being...comprising...three hypostases" is therefore equivalent to the expression *a person comprising three persons*. But what does this mean? Is this not a combination of words that is devoid of all conceivable content? We find such a strange formula for the concept of God neither in Christianity nor in any other religion.

In fact, Christianity defines God as one entity or nature (essence, nature; *ousia, physis*) in three inseparable hypostases, or persons. Even though this concept surpasses the ordinary human understanding, which moves in the domain of finite things, it contains a determinate thought that is free of logical contradiction and fully satisfies the higher demands of speculation. In any case, the Christian concept of God as a triune essence, eternal and all-perfect, has very strained relations with Professor Vvedensky's "second characteristic." For a goal presupposes imperfection in one who strives toward it, and activity presupposes a time in which it occurs. One should not forget that, according to Christian doctrine, the "form of a servant" (Phil. 2:7) veils the deity in the second subject (hypostasis) of the Holy Trinity, the logos. It is this hypostasis which has the most immediate connection to the world; this is by virtue of the Incarnation, which is pre-initiated for all eternity and pre-initiated from all eternity. To *this* hypostasis one can, without any contradiction, refer all religious anthropopathisms, but from this one can by no means draw an inference to the very concept of God in essence, as did the Monophysite-Theopaschites, who

---

8. Besides meaning "person," the Russian word *litso* can also mean "countenance" or "face."—TR.

asserted that the Deity itself had suffered and died on the cross.[9]

Professor Vvedensky justly remarks that the right of the thinking mind to transform or "restructure" given religious concepts must have a limit. There is no doubt about that: A serious thinker will not attach just any content to a generally accepted term, nor will he take a certain word to mean just anything at all. But it is much more difficult to find here a real limit, obligatory for the mind, than Professor Vvedensky thinks. In any case, it is impossible to accept the limit that he has indicated. In the fundamental Christian teaching, the earlier religious concepts of God had already undergone radical restructuring even as regards what appears untouchable for Professor Vvedensky. According to the Christian conception, God's essential characteristic is absolute perfection not only in the moral but also in the metaphysical sense. That is, God must inevitably transcend all limitations; in particular, He must transcend time and therefore that discrete purposive activity which is conceivable only in time but which Professor Vvedensky decisively attributes to God as such, and therefore to the Christian God.

But I will not insist on this unwitting contradiction between Professor Vvedensky's view and some of the foundations of the Christian teaching. In his further discussion, Professor Vvedensky, having begun by referring to all religions without excep-

9. According to the Orthodox definition, by virtue of the true union of the two natures in Christ one can say that God suffered, died, and rose from the dead precisely in the sense that the one who suffered, died, and rose from the dead was the true God. But one cannot say that Deity itself or the divine nature suffered, died, and rose from the dead. That would be both absurd and wicked. In short, the Orthodox formula against the Monophysite formula consists in the fact that Christ suffered, died, and rose from the dead *not according to His divinity but according to His humanity.*—Solovyov's note.

tion, comes—imperceptibly for himself and unexpectedly for the reader—to an assertion that annuls all religions without exception.

IV

Although I consider wholly unjustified the accusation that Spinoza's philosophy is atheistic, I hasten to point out that this accusation, as it is expressed by Professor Vvedensky, has nothing in common with those odious personal attacks to which the Amsterdam philosopher was often subjected for his so-called "atheism." Professor Vvedensky, remaining unflaggingly at the high level of the theoretical discussion of ideas, makes the careful, detailed qualification that, personally, Spinoza was not an atheist, that his temper was a religious one, but that, developing Descartes' system in a one-sided, mechanical direction, he arrived at views that excluded the concept of God, while retaining, by a *conscientious* illusion, the word "God" to designate an object that bears no resemblance to God. Whether this was really the case with regard to Spinoza—we shall consider below. At present, we must observe that something happened to Professor Vvedensky himself that is similar to what he tells us about Spinoza. Remaining on the same purely theoretical, or intellectual, ground and not doubting the sincere personal devotion of Professor Vvedensky to religious interests and Christian principles, we find that a one-sided and rectilinear development of Kantian ideas unwittingly led him to opinions that take away from religion in general its essential content and distinctive character, its *raison d'être*. In particular, he writes the following:

[T]he concept God does not refer to an object which is given in experience. If it referred to such an object, it would, of course, have to correspond to its object, and if there was a lack of correspondence, philosophy would have the right to modify the concept, without changing its name. But in the concept God we conceive not what is given in experience, but what satisfies our religious needs, and in which as a consequence we *merely believe* as though it existed (the italics are Solovyov's— Trans.). And when later we encounter philosophy, we turn to it, needless to say, with the question of whether we are right in our belief, that is, whether what we believe in exists.[10]

It thus turns out that, as long as we "merely believe" in God, we do not yet know whether He actually exists. Although it is the case in religion that we believe, nonetheless nothing guarantees—according to Professor Vvedensky—the actual existence of the object of our belief, and we must turn for such a guarantee to philosophy, which, without examining the essence or content of our religious concepts, considers only the question of whether or not the actual objects corresponding to these concepts exist. I confess that, in reading such an assertion, I had the impression that Professor Vvedensky was discussing something that was occurring on the rings of Saturn or on Mercury, where all things perhaps happen in a manner opposite to what we know from our terrestrial experience. I will not, of course, appeal to my own experience. But in the domain of religion, as in other domains of the human spirit, there are recognized "experts," whose testimony about certain questions has a decisive significance, inde-

10. Vvedensky, "The Atheism of Spinoza's Philosophy," p. 8.

pendent of any personal opinions. Here, for example, is the "testimony of an expert," which I present only in this capacity, irrespective of his sacred authority: "That which *was* from the beginning, which we have heard, which we have *seen* with our eyes, which we have *looked upon*, and our hands have *handled*, of the Word of life: (For the life was *manifested*, and we have *seen* it, and *bear witness*, and shew unto you that eternal life, which was with the Father, and was *manifested* unto us); That which we have *seen* and *heard*, declare we unto you, that ye also may have fellowship unto us; and truly our fellowship is with the Father, and with his Son Jesus Christ" (1 John 1:1–3).[11]

V

According to Professor Vvedensky, the concept of God does not refer to an object given in experience. The apostle John the Divine particularly insists on the fact that his concept of God refers to an object given in experience even for the external senses. To be sure, one cannot see, hear, or touch the very being of God, but that is impossible as regards any being as such. We sensuously experience only the *manifested* effects of entities, which for us serve as signs and expressions of their being and inner nature.

Independently of the Kantian concept of experience, which I consider erroneous, I by no means deny the important differences between religious experience and that experience in which objects of the physical world are given to us. But with reference to what we are discussing here, those two forms of experience coincide completely. Our conviction that the sun actually exists is inseparable from the optical and thermal sensations which we

11. The italics are Solovyov's.—Tr.

ascribe to the action of this object. Through these sensations we become certain of the reality of the sun's existence and do not require any confirmation of this certainty from astronomical theories. In fact, no astronomy could prove to us the sun's existence if we took the standpoint of subjective idealism, or illusionism. The task of science as regards this object consists only in giving us new, clearer, more precise, and more complete concepts of that combination of phenomena which we call the sun. The question of whether some reality that exists outside our consciousness corresponds to these phenomena and concepts, this question of the *existence of the object*, is in no wise posed or resolved by science, which is concerned only with the *relationships among phenomena*. Both the most learned astronomer and the most ignorant savage accept the objective existence of celestial bodies *on faith*.

All the telescopic observations, spectral analyses, and mathematical calculations in the world will not give a single serious argument for the real existence of the sun if this scientist makes up his mind to accept the point of view of subjective idealism. For all these scientific riches find a perfect place within the limits of the concept of a celestial body as a phenomenon connected with other phenomena according to a strictly determined order *within our consciousness*, without the slightest connection with anything outside it.[12]

12. Predictions of eclipses and other such triumphs of exact science could refute only the point of view of "voluntarism" or "arbitrarism" (a view that is, incidentally, supported by no one), according to which phenomena occur any which way, due to the blind and unconnected whim of the active force or forces. But the triumphs of science have no relation whatsoever to subjective idealism, according to which the world of phenomena is a *rigorously ordered* and *regular system* of hallucinations. To think that correct predictions speak in favor of the reality of these phenomena is to presuppose the real significance of time, i.e., that which remains to be proven.— Solovyov's note.

Notwithstanding all the differences here in other respects, what we have said about the certainty of the physical sun's existence is also fully applicable to the question of the certainty of the spiritual sun's existence. The fact that we are certain of the actual existence of the Deity is inseparably linked with the phenomena which are given to us in religious experience and which we ascribe to the action of the Deity upon us. This is true for all religions. The ancient Greeks would not have believed in the existence of Dionysus if they had not experienced his psycho-corporeal action in their states of inebriation. Belief in the Christian God is based on His full manifestation in mankind's historical experience. And although this experience had its most intense and concentrated expression in the events of Christ's earthly life, it is, of course, not exhausted by these events. No one will deny the actual religious experience of the Apostle Paul, St. Francis of Assisi, or St. Sergius of Radonezh. Finally, there is also indirect religious experience, which involves belief in what others report, the life of tradition, ancestral and spiritual solidarity. One can remark the same thing with regard to objects of the physical world. I do not use a telescope, but by no means do I question the actual existence of the planet Neptune and other celestial bodies that are invisible to the naked eye.

If the certainty that the object of religion actually exists is based on religious *experience*, the task of philosophy in this connection can consist only in transforming and extending this experience, that is, in making our *concepts* of facts given in actual religion more precise, clear, and complete. Philosophy can investigate religious objects but, by itself, it can neither create them nor certify their existence for us, just as astronomy cannot do this with regard to celestial bodies. Against this it would be useless to point to the so-called proofs of God's existence, which are partly based on logical errors, as Kant has demonstrated, and which partly (especially the teleological and moral proofs) rely on data of external and internal experience and thus confirm our thesis. To be sure, our certainty that the objects of religion exist is not limited to the data of our religious experience, but it is just as indubitable that this certainty is based on these data and cannot exist without them, just as the certainty of our astronomical knowledge does not wholly depend on what we see and observe in the heavens but is indubitably based only on such observations.

A clear illustration of this is Le Verrier's famous discovery.[13] In the first place, this discovery was conditioned by observational data concerning other planets and by calculations of their orbits on the basis of these observations. Secondly, the further mathematical calculations and combinations that led the Parisian astronomer to infer the necessary existence of the new planet could not, in themselves, certify the actual existence of this planet, since this planet, like the "counter-earth" of the Pythagoreans, could have turned out to be an erroneous inference. Le Verrier's work received its true significance only through empirical verification, that is, when the new planet was actually observed through a telescope. In fact, many astronomers discover new asteroids and comets every year, and the fact of their observation provides complete certainty as to the existence of these bodies. In general, the main role in the successes of astronomy indubitably belongs to the telescope and to spectral analysis, that is, to improved methods of observation and experimentation. If the so-called proofs of God's existence could indicate the conditions under which we could have new

---

13. Knowledge of the perturbations of Uranus led the French astronomer Urbain Le Verrier (1811–1877) to infer the existence of a new planet, Neptune.—TR.

perceptions of divine objects, just as Le Verrier's calculations indicated to astronomers where they should point their telescopes in order to catch sight of the new planet, then these proofs would, of course, have major significance for the formation of religious convictions.

VI

In contrast to theoretical discussions of religious objects, every actual religion unfailingly recognizes the Deity, i.e., the supreme object of worship or religious feeling, as given in experience. That is the first characteristic of this concept, a characteristic that does not face the risk of encountering any *instantia contrarii*. Nirvana, the venerated goal toward which Buddhist sages strive, is, for these sages, not an abstract concept but something that has already been experienced by others and that, potentially, is something that these sages themselves can experience. To feel the absolute in oneself as unconditional *detachment* from all determinations is that state of inner experience which gives to Buddhism its entire religious content, thereby distinguishing it from other religions as well as from theoretical discussions of the infinite. The all-soul of the Brahmins is known in the actual experience of the inner concentration of all human powers, of man's entire psychophysical being, which, in this concentration, is truly united and truly coincides with the very object of this religion. And in this "identity of subject and object," a human being essentially experiences absolute Deity. Many people have experienced the religious experience of pantheism—the inner perception or sensation of one's identity with the all-one substance of the world. Not having experienced anything like this, thinkers of exclusive and superficial rationality call such an empirically given state "fanaticism" or "fantasy."

But we can disregard this, especially if we remember that, for many people, every religion, and even every "metaphysics," is fanaticism, fantasy, and superstition.

The pantheistic sense of communion with the all-one substance, producing entire religious doctrines, also fills with profound religious inspiration the world-view of such thinkers as Spinoza and Goethe. In distant Asia, pantheism is a popular religion, while in Europe it has long been the favorite religion of metaphysicians and poets, for whom it is not an abstract concept but a given of experience.

But there is something even more important and remarkable: based on religious experience, the ideas of the absolute as complete detachment from all determinations (Buddhism) and as the all-one substance of all being (Brahmanism) have indubitably entered, as subordinate elements, into the more content-rich Christian vision, based on a more profound and perfect religious experience (in the true Revelation). I am speaking not of various mystical and Gnostic heresies, which wished to elevate this Eastern element from a subordinate one to the dominant one and to restore paganism beneath a Christian shell, but of perfectly orthodox and ecclesiastically authoritative writers—theologians, mystics, and ascetics. Let me mention first those works which, because of their high worth, were attributed to a figure from the apostolic age, St. Dionysius the Areopagite, and as early as the fifth century received a generally recognized authority in the church; secondly, the writings of the profound and learned commentator on these works, St. Maximus Confessor, who suffered for orthodoxy in the struggle with the Monothelitic heresy; and finally, various works of ascetic writers, both ancient and more recent, which have been compiled in collections of varying size with the general title *Philokalia*. Of course, this literature is not a complete expression of Christianity; it expresses only one of the aspects of Christianity. But the widespread character and authority of these writings indubitably prove that the aspect of Christianity which they express has an essential significance for Christianity, and that this aspect must necessarily be considered when defining the Christian concept of God.

In this connection one should note a certain fundamental traditional point of view in which all the writers mentioned follow the Areopagite. According to them, the correct concept of God is established in two ways: (1) through the consistent and absolute denial that God has any attributes (this is called *theologia apofatike*) and (2) through the attribution to God of all positive qualities in the highest degree or in their absolute potency (*theologia katafatike*).

The presumed Areopagite would, of course, not have been received into the true Areopagus of church fathers and teachers if his mystical views were as remote from positive Christianity as Spinoza's pantheism. Nevertheless, I have the strong apprehension that this highly authoritative church theologian has, in his ideas about God, a greater inner kinship with the Amsterdam philosopher than with the Petersburg one. I do not say this as a reproach. Professor Vvedensky has a perfect, inalienable right to prefer analytically rational concepts of God to the ideas of contemplative mysticism. He can be reproached only when he turns this right into a general obligation, excluding *implicite* from the Christian religion an element that indubitably belongs to it, even if this element does not meet the requirements of one or another philosophizing mind.

VII

We are in complete agreement with Professor Vvedensky that our logical right to understand the concept of God in our own way must have a limit, which depends on the essential content of the actual religions. But we have found that the limit indicated by Professor Vvedensky does not coincide with the actual limit, and that the invariable characteristics of the concept of Deity that he proposes must be modified if one wishes to make this concept applicable to all religions. First of all, one must restore an attribute that Professor Vvedensky omits and apparently even rejects: the grounding of the concept in actual religious experience. It is this characteristic that distinguishes this concept as a religious one, i.e., as a concept that expresses a living relation to the object, from abstract discussions of the object. Then, of the characteristics proposed by Professor Vvedensky, one must accept only the first. Indisputably, the idea of God contains the concept of superiority to man, just as religion itself, by its concept, is worship or veneration, which presupposes the superiority of its object. To be sure, one can speak of superiority here only in certain respects and to certain degrees. Professor Vvedensky appears to restrict this characteristic unduly when he considers it impossible to see God in such objects as "matter" or a "hurricane." *Actual* matter and an actual hurricane have been and are objects of divine worship. However, it is possible that Professor Vvedensky had in mind only the conceptions and hypotheses of chemists and physicists about matter and its phenomena, which, of course, produce ideas of the Deity in no one. These pedestrian myths, created by one-sided minds, clearly are not superior to man *in any respect*, which one can say neither about actual matter nor even about an actual hurricane.

As for the second characteristic, personal conscious will and purposive action, it must be modified radically. If Professor Vvedensky could express his view in a negative form where the Deity should not be conceived as *impersonal, will-less, uncon-*

scious, and *acting without purpose*—then we would agree with him at once and offer only some clarifications of this thesis.

To acknowledge God as impersonal, will-less, and so forth is impossible because that would be to place him below man, or to deny a necessary characteristic of Deity: superiority to man. By justifiably regarding such objects as, for instance, furniture, paving stones, logs, and sand heaps will-less, impersonal, and unconscious, we affirm the superiority to them of man's personal, conscious, and purposively acting being. And no sophistries could alter such an axiomatic judgment of ours. To acknowledge the Deity as impersonal or will-less in this case would be to lower it to the level of inferior things that have not attained the general and elementary advantages of man's nature. And we decisively affirm that no pagan religions or pantheistic philosophies have ever succumbed to such an obvious absurdity. But Professor Vvedensky mistakenly thinks that the impossibility of considering the Deity impersonal leads to the necessity of acknowledging the Deity to be personal. Or, speaking the language of formal logic, he erroneously sees a contradictory relationship where it is a question of relative opposition; he erroneously sees a dilemma where *datur tertium quid.*

VIII

The words "person" and "personhood" by no means have the firmly fixed meaning that Professor Vvedensky appears to ascribe to them. Without mentioning the Roman terminology, where *persona* signified nothing more than a *mask,* at the present time the corresponding word in all languages is used in two quite distinct senses. On the one hand, when it is a question of personal dignity, rights, freedom, and so forth, personhood is understood as a positive principle of independence which belongs to man as a spiritual being, in contradistinction to the negative properties of passive, inert material being. But if human personhood is thus opposed to lower impersonal nature, then, on the other hand, personal character is opposed to man's higher dignity and purpose, when we say, for example: *c'est un homme personnel* or *er ist nur einer persönlichen Gesinnung fähig*. The meaning of such expressions becomes clear when we compare them with the Gospel saying: He who finds his soul shall lose it; he who loses his soul shall find it.[14] Of course, this salvific loss of the soul is understood to mean not the transformation of a human being into a soulless thing, not the suicide of his metaphysical essence, but only the moral stifling of his egoism. What the Gospel calls "soul," what we usually call our "I," our personhood, is not a full self-enclosed circle of life possessing its own content, essence, or meaning of being, but only a bearer or *support (hypostasis)* of something other and higher. Surrendering himself to this other, forgetting about his own I, a human being appears to lose himself, to sacrifice himself. But, in fact, he asserts himself in his true significance and purpose, and fills his personal life with a true content, something with which his personal life becomes inseparably merged. He thus transforms his personal life into eternal life. By contrast, by directing his psychic energies toward his own soul taken separately, by taking the support of life for the content of life and the bearer for the goal, i.e., by surrendering himself to egoism, a human being loses his soul, his real personhood, casting it into emptiness or contentlessness. Egoism is only an imaginary self-assertion of human

14. This conveys in a compact form the general content of the following Gospel texts: Matt. 10:39 and 16:25; Mark 8:35; Luke 9:24, and 17:33; John 12:25.—Solovyov's note. [The Russian Gospels have "dusha" ("soul") where the King James Version has "life."]

personhood; personhood actually asserts itself only when it sur-
renders itself willingly and consciously to something else that is
higher. Egoism is, in fact, the separation of personhood from its
life-content, the separation of the support, or hypostasis, of
being from its essence (*ousia*), a rupture between existence and
its goal, between external fact and inner value, between that
which lives and that for the sake of which it is worth living. Such
a separation of the self-oriented I from its life-essence is, without doubt, the moral death and perdition of the soul.

But if our personhood's independence and content are
therefore only formal in character, and our personhood gains
essential independence and content only when it affirms itself as
the support of something else higher than it, then is it correct to
transfer a concept abstracted from our personal life to this
higher thing, in which our personhood can and must preserve
itself only by surrendering itself to this higher thing and enter-
ing with it into a fullness of union not yet experienced by us?
Should not this higher thing, i.e., Deity, necessarily be recognized as *suprapersonal*? To be sure, one can object that, even
though Deity is suprapersonal with respect to *us*, to *our personhood*, it is nevertheless personal in itself. But this amounts to the
assertion that, apart from its relation to us, Deity is personal in
the same way we are. However, this kind of anthropopathic concept of God can, it appears, be applied only to the lower forms
of pagan religions, and what right do we have to demand from a
philosopher that he make his concepts conform to the concepts
of polytheists? If we exclude from the concept of personhood all
the empirical content that does not suit the Deity of the mono-
theists, then no concrete positive features will remain in this
concept, and we will get only logical positiveness through a
series of double negations: Deity is *not impersonal, not unconscious, not will-less*, and so forth. And given the impossibility of

connecting with this determination any data of self-observation and psychological analysis, all these double negations can be replaced by the positing not of personal but of suprapersonal being. The most positively religious man, to whom all philosophical pantheism is alien, will at once understand us and agree with us if we tell him that, although the Deity may think, it thinks in a wholly other way than we; that, although it may have consciousness and will, they are wholly unlike the ones we have; and so forth. But in calling Deity suprapersonal, we only express all these religious axioms with a single word, and this word represents a desirable logical limit which encloses the concept of God, protecting it both from confusion with the concept of soulless, inert being and from the just as lamentable confusion with the concept of man's empirical personhood. In characterizing Deity as suprapersonal, we do not give occasion for any misunderstandings, whereas in ascribing a personal character to the all-encompassing entity, which is not subordinate to time and is therefore unchanging, etc., we are unquestionably playing with words and falling into that very same *quaternio terminorum* which Professor Vvedensky is so afraid of.

IX

Although the characteristic of suprapersonhood is more clearly manifested at the higher stages of religious development, it is also present at all the lower stages, giving us the right to accept it as a general characteristic of the very concept of God. Despite the anthropomorphic and anthropopathic character of the pagan deities, not one of these deities is distinctly viewed as a personal entity, i.e., as an entity that is not wholly determined by its given nature but can be free of this nature. Stone-worship, tree-worship, and animal-worship are genuine religious cults, but can one really find personhood in their objects, i.e., in the entities that are always connected with this stone, tree, or animal? And, in the higher forms of pagan religion, is it really the case that Helios sends his rays because he wants to, and not because he has a light-bearing, solar nature? Is it the case that Hades abides in the underground realm instead of on Olympus because of his free preference and decision, and not because his nature is that of a netherworld entity? Can one seriously consider the great many-breasted Ephesian Artemis, who gives birth to and feeds all plants and all animals without exception, to be a person who acts purposively, consciously, and on the basis of free will? Or can one seriously consider Isis, who is something intermediate between the moon and a cow, to be such a person? Clearly, in all these entities, nature and spirit, fateful necessity and freedom, are so closely interconnected that it is impossible to apply our concepts of personhood to this connection. And if we cannot consider these entities impersonal and if their nature surpasses ours in strength and endurance, we must concede to them a certain share of suprapersonhood.

The higher human consciousness enriched by both the individual and the collective religious experience of mankind rises, the clearer becomes the need to understand the fundamental object of this experience as suprapersonal. This necessity is emphasized in the basic Christian dogmas, i.e., the dogmas of the Trinity and the Incarnation. Every personal entity as such has only a single personhood, and a single entity with three persons is therefore a suprapersonal entity. Furthermore, if, in Himself, God were already a person as Professor Vvedensky understands this term, i.e., in the human sense, there would be no need of any particular humanization and incarnation of God: An essentially personal God could be accessible to man, could reveal Himself to man and enter with man into any relations whatever, while remaining Himself and not "becoming flesh," not adding human nature to Himself.

X

Material nature is impersonal. Personhood is a specific characteristic of man. In itself, or as the absolute, Deity is suprapersonal. On this point pantheism and even Buddhistic negativism converge with both Christian teaching and the requirements of philosophical speculation. The concept of the Deity as such, or the concept of the absolute, is *one and the same* from all these points of view. Asiatic and European mystics, Alexandrian Platonists and Hebrew Kaballists, church fathers and independent thinkers, Persian Sufis and Italian monks, Cardinal Nicholas of Cusa and Jacob Boehme, Pseudo-Dionysius and Spinoza, Maximus the Confessor and Schelling—all confess, with one heart and one voice, the inconceivable and ineffable absoluteness of the Deity.

There is no disagreement about the fundamental, primordial concept of the absolute as such. Disagreement begins only with those secondary determinations of Deity which are logically conditioned by the relation of Deity to everything that is not itself.

Deity as the absolute is not conditioned by anything apart from itself (it is *causa sui*), and it also conditions everything (it is *causa omnium*). Everything that exists has in Deity the ultimate or definitive foundation of its being, its substance. This concept of God as the one substance of all things, which logically follows from the very concept of His absoluteness or genuine divinity (since if the unconditional foundation of anything whatever were found outside God, it would limit Him and thereby annul His Deity), this truth of the all-one substance, confessed under different names by pagans, is confessed by Christians (in harmony with Jews and Moslems) under the true name God Almighty. Spinoza made an entire philosophical system out of this fundamental and necessary part of our creed. To call his philosophy an atheism because it does not go beyond this part of our creed would be nearly as unjust as to assert that Euclid was not a mathematician because he did not consider analysis and the differential calculus but limited himself to elementary geometry, or that Kepler was not an astronomer because he limited himself to the statics of the solar system and did not consider its origin or other star systems.

To be sure, the fact that Spinoza did not go beyond the concept of absolute substance led him to commit certain serious errors. Seeing in everything that exists only general properties and relations, derived *a priori*, *more geometrico*, from the concept of the being and thinking of the infinite substance, he considered this substance to be the direct generating cause of everything that exists. By no means denying the proper absolute life of God Almighty, Spinoza characterized Him at the same time as the *natura naturans* of our world of phenomena, understood realistically as *natura naturata*, or as an expression—adequate in its combination—of the absolute first cause. Despite the total incorrectness of such a view, an incorrectness that is perfectly clear now to our minds, we must not forget that, *philosophically*, this view could be truly removed only by critical idealism, which showed that, between the absolute entity (assuming the existence of such an entity) and the world of phenomena, there is certainly a subject of knowledge, who, if only by the exclusively formal character of its functions, cannot be recognized as absolute. This point of view destroys Spinozism as a philosophical system, as a complete explanation of the world, but it does not turn it into an atheism.

XI

Even more significant is another one-sided element in Spinoza's philosophy, or a deficiency in his concept of God as *only* the absolute substance. Besides the general constant and self-identical properties and relations of objects, the actual world also has something opposite to this: development, process. This world not only exists, but something is being done or happening in it. In addition to the static aspect of the world's being, there is also a dynamic, or historical, aspect. But if the idea of the absolute substance links the world's being and essence with Deity, this idea does not give any foundation for the world's *becoming* (*genesis*, *Werden*). It does not bring the historical aspect of the world and mankind into any kind of positive relationship with Deity. As soon as the significance of this side of universal life is acknowledged and understood, Spinoza's static pantheism ceases to satisfy both the religious sense and philosophical thought. God cannot only be a god of geometry and physics. He must also be a god of history. But in Spinoza's system there is as little place for the god of history as in the system of the Eleatics. Many critics have reproached Spinoza for this deficiency. But it would be unjust to repeat these reproaches without the following essential qualifications.

(1) Outside the Jewish and Christian religions and certain isolated philosophical views, we do not find the presence of the historical element in any other religious or philosophical system. Most believers and thinkers do not understand the cumulative changes of the world historically as a single process through which something new is becoming or happening, a process with a determinate positive meaning and direction. Nowhere in paganism was Deity understood as the god of history. Without mentioning the typical anti-historical views of Hindu and Chinese religio-philosophical wisdom, in lands far-

ther West as well we encounter only either complete stasis (as in the case of the petrified deities of the Egyptians or the Ephesian Artemis) or constant but fruitless movement (as in the case of Homer's Olympians). The pagan lack of historical understanding has been preserved in the dual faith of the Christian nations. And, even in European science, the concept of a single, determinate historical process began to appear only a hundred years after Spinoza. In any case, one cannot attach the name atheism to the absence in the concept of God of an element that was foreign to the majority of religious and metaphysical doctrines.

(2) We acknowledge in Deity the absolute fullness of life. We connect the cosmic and historical process with Deity. We find in Deity the final ground both for the collective history of mankind and for the personal history of every human soul. We affirm the decisive presence of Deity in all the events of cosmic and private life; here, we acknowledge everything as *non sine numine factum*.[15] But this concerns precisely only fact, whereas the mode of the divine presence—*quomodo factum*—may be completely unknown for us. We only know that this mode is worthy of the Deity, or corresponds to Deity's absolute essence. We know that Deity as such participates in the cosmic and historical process *in a divine manner*. An increasing fullness of the perception of the real presence of the divine in everything that is human is given in (Christian) Revelation, but here too only the human aspect increases. To us is given the fact of the perfect union of the divine and human natures in Christ, and we can understand the whole rational necessity or the whole meaning of this fact. But the mode, the *quomodo*, of the union could not be revealed to us, and is accessible to us only "through a glass, darkly." In any case, God is the god of history not according to

---

15. "Not made without divine inspiration."—Tr.

His Deity but according to His humanity, and, as a consequence, the absence of a historical aspect in the concept of God only makes a philosopher a non-Christian, not an atheist.

Once the historical process is conceived as a certain relationship of two aspects, divine and human, which are jointly present in this process, then by no means can every condition and characteristic of the process taken *in concreto* be directly transferred to one of the aspects, namely the divine one, taken in itself or separately. One should not be carried away by the analogy of the historical process with ordinary human activity. For instance, from the fact that, in participating in the historical process, man acts in a purposive manner it cannot be concluded that the Deity, also participating in this process, must also act purposively. In essence, that would be as unfounded as to conclude from the analogous action of sunlight and the light of a kerosene lamp that the sun, like the lamp, could be lit by Swedish matches.

(3) Let us note, in conclusion, that, although the concept of Deity as the absolute substance is insufficient for a religio-historical view, such a view requires this concept. In fact, only by understanding the Deity as the absolute substance, as the Almighty, can we feel the logical necessity of connecting with the Deity all the aspects of existence and therefore historical becoming as well. And if we did not understand the Deity as absolute or all-one, we, like the deists, could calmly suppose that God and the world with all its history exist apart from each other. It appears indubitable to me that Spinoza's static pantheism was necessary as a presupposition for the appearance of Hegel's historical pantheism, and then of positive Christian philosophy.

XII

I still have to say a few words about Professor Vvedensky's attempt to explain why Spinoza, despite being a religiously oriented philosopher, created an atheistic philosophy. The true culprit, it turns out, is Descartes. Professor Vvedensky states the following:

> Of course, in Descartes we find not merely the name but also the concept of God; for Descartes' God, no matter how he defined him in his little model of geometrical exposition, acts purposively, for example, refrains from deception, and is not simply a blind, even if infinite, substance. But it is well known that this God played only a subsidiary role in Descartes: by means of this concept he connected what he could not connect in any other way, much as Anaxagoras made use of the concept of reason only when he could not explain a thing mechanistically. As Windelband justly observes: "Descartes would have used the concept of matter in the same way as that of God if it could have rendered him the same service as the latter." And is it not strange that a philosophy in which the concept of God plays a subsidiary role, and which could readily get along without it, should necessarily have paved the way for pantheism, rather than something else. Is it not clear that it could just as easily have paved the way for atheism? Let us not forget that La Mettrie in developing his materialism quoted Descartes more consistently than any other writer.[16]

16. Aleksandr Vvedensky, "The Atheism of Spinoza's Philosophy," p. 21.

Further on, Vvedensky adds:

> However, anyone who carries out with complete consis-
> tency the identification of real and logical relations and,
> with Descartes, regards all effects and states of affairs as
> [logical] consequences and all causes as [logical]
> grounds, must also adopt the purely mechanistic world-
> view which flows from this identification and must carry
> it out with even greater consistency than Descartes him-
> self did. And in that case substance, becoming one, loses
> all purposive action, and everything in it turns into the
> logically necessary consequences of its nature; that is, it
> no longer fits the concept God. It was by such a path that
> Descartes' philosophy paved the way for the atheism of
> Spinoza's doctrine. This depended on the fact that the
> identification of real and logical relations that began
> with Descartes and was consistently carried out by
> Spinoza led to a purely mechanistic world-view, fully
> accepted by Spinoza.[17]

Without examining the question of whether Spinoza's philosophy, with its infinitely thinking substance, can be characterized as a purely mechanistic world-view, and without touching
on Professor Vvedensky's decisive but enigmatic assertion that
the identification of real relations with logical ones inevitably
leads to a purely mechanistic representation of the world, I will
only point out the fundamental internal contradiction in this
entire explanation. If Descartes' system contained the possibility of being developed and reworked in a theistic direction, or
in any case, a direction that was not atheistic, and Malebranche,
who was a religious person, developed his teacher's philosophy

17. Ibid, pp. 22–23.

precisely in this direction, then why did Spinoza, who was also a religious person and by no means an atheist, not act in a like manner? In virtue of what necessity did Spinoza take from Descartes only what inevitably led to atheism, something which was foreign to his personal feelings and views? Why did he not leave the development of the atheistic elements of Cartesianism to people who were inclined to that by nature, like the later materialistic thinker La Mettrie, to whom Professor Vvedensky refers? For, in general, disciples take and develop from the ideas of their teachers that which most suits them. For instance, several theologians and pietists among the Hegelians transformed their teacher's system into a philosophical commentary on orthodox Lutheran theology, whereas their colleagues of another bent derived the most radical atheism from the same system. And so with regard to Spinoza's system too it is impossible to avoid the dilemma: either he derived from Cartesianism precisely an atheistic (and not some other) view because, by his personal convictions and sentiments, he was inclined to atheism (which even Professor Vvedensky does not assert); or Spinoza's philosophy was not at all atheistic, but essentially conformed to the religiously-contemplative, pantheistic tenor of his mind.

⁂

Despite all its incompleteness and imperfection, the concept of God that Spinoza's philosophy gives us meets the first necessary requirement of the true worship of and thinking about God. Many religious people have found spiritual sustenance in this philosophy. And the present brief apology is inspired first of all by gratitude for how Spinozism served me in the transitional period of my youth—with respect to religion as well as philosophy. In conclusion, I must express my sincere gratitude to the esteemed Professor Vvedensky as well, who, with his clear and interesting formulation of the question, provoked me to repay, without delaying further, at least part of an old debt.

www.ingramcontent.com/pod-product-compliance
Lightning Source LLC
Chambersburg PA
CBHW021506090426
42739CB00007B/484